Eight Special Nights

Eight Special Nights

Naftali
in the
BEIS HAMIKDASH
SERIES

A young boy and
his classmates live
through the miracles
of Chanukah

*A historical adventure, including
the laws of kiddush HaShem,
kiddush ha-chodesh, and
lighting the Menorah*

by Yaakov Meir Strauss

FELDHEIM PUBLISHERS
JERUSALEM · NEW YORK

Originally published in Hebrew as *HaMelech Shav L'Veiso* (5772)

Translated into English by Brocha David
Typeset by Eden Chachamtzedek

Also by the author:
Three Special Days (Jerusalem: Feldheim Publishers, 2003)
Seven Special Weeks (Jerusalem: Feldheim Publishers, 2005)
One Special Prayer (Jerusalem: Feldheim Publishers, 2007)
The King's Special Loaves (Jerusalem: Feldheim Publishers, 2009)
Special Days of Joy (Jerusalem: Feldheim Publishers, 2019)

English edition (hardcover), first published: 2020

Paperback edition:
ISBN 978-1-68025-534-8

DISTRIBUTED BY:
Feldheim Publishers
POB 43163 / Jerusalem, Israel
208 Airport Executive Park
Nanuet, NY 10954
www.feldheim.com

DISTRIBUTED IN EUROPE BY:
Lehmanns
+44-0-191-430-0333
info@lehmanns.co.uk
www.lehmanns.co.uk

DISTRIBUTED IN AUSTRALIA BY:
Golds World of Judaica
+613 95278775
info@golds.com.au
www.golds.com.au

Printed in the USA

ציון לנפש חיה

In loving memory
of a righteous woman

מרת **חוה שטראוס** ע"ה

בת הרה"ח ר' **אברהם וועג** יבלחט"א

She raised and educated her children to
love of Torah and pure fear of Hashem
with much self-sacrifice and devotion.

She was a full partner to her husband,
the author, in the publication of this series.

She passed on to the World of Truth
on 16 Sivan 5778.

ת.נ.צ.ב.ה.

Berachah received from

HaRav HaGaon
Rabbi Chayim Kanievsky, shlita

upon his perusal of HaMelech Shav L'Veiso,
the sixth Hebrew volume in the
"Naftali in the Beis HaMikdash" series:

הספר "המלך שב לביתו"
השישי מסדרת הספרים "בחצרות בית ה'"
היה למראה עיני

מרן הגאון ר' **חיים קניבסקי** שליט"א
ונהנה מהספר מאוד ואמר:

"זה דבר טוב מאד ויהיה לתועלת"
ובירך: "שיהיה ברכה והצלחה"

Contents

Key to Charts and Maps xi

Dear Reader xiii

The BeChatzros Beis Hashem Institute xv

Chapter One
In the Middle
of the Night 1

Chapter Two
Matters of
Life and Death 11

Chapter Three
Thirty-Eight
Compartments 21

Chapter Four
The Missing
Miniature 33

Chapter Five
Feast of the
Faithful 46

Chapter Six
In Search of
the Miniature 55

Chapter Seven
A Special Lesson 62

Chapter Eight
Narrow Escape 69

Chapter Nine
Moon Watching 81

Chapter Ten
Against the Odds 92

Chapter Eleven
Return of Augustus 103

Chapter Twelve
Battle Cries 110

Chapter Thirteen
The Wood Offering 117

Chapter Fourteen
Mizbeach under
Construction 123

Chapter Fifteen
The Ancient Flute 131

Chapter Sixteen
Discovery in
the Oil Chamber 143

Chapter Seventeen
The Iron Menorah 151

Chapter Eighteen
Bright Idea 160

Chapter Nineteen
Song in the Cellar 170

Chapter Twenty
The Miracle of
the Oil Jug 179

Chapter Twenty-One

Preparing the Lamps 188

Chapter Twenty-Two

Reuven Comes Home 197

Chapter Twenty-Three

The King Comes Home 207

Key to Reference Numbers, Charts, and Maps of Sites in the Beis HaMikdash 217

Glossary 223

On pages 217–221, you will find a complete list of every item in the Beis HaMikdash, and on page 232 there is a map showing the *Ezras Nashim* and the *Azarah*.

Key to Charts and Maps

The Ulam (Antechamber), Heichal (Temple Chamber),
and Kodesh HaKodashim (Holy of Holies) 27

The Compartments 29

The Compartments (Side View) 31

The Kohanim's Entrance into the Heichal 39

The Staircase 43

The Compartments, Staircase, and Drainage Channel 44

Temple Mount 134

The Azarah 137

Ezras Nashim 147

How the Mizbeach Was Built 198

The Mizbeach and Its Ramps 198

The Punishments for Mishmeres Bilgah 205

Ezras Nashim and Azarah 232

Dear Reader

EIGHT SPECIAL NIGHTS is a work of historical fiction. The book relives the Chanukah miracles through the eyes of an ancestor of our hero, Naftali, after whom he was named. Interwoven are exciting sub-plots full of intrigue and suspense, excitement and surprise. The story takes place in the middle of the Second Temple period.

Much thought and care has gone into making sure that the details are accurate and based on Torah sources. However, because the author has tried to bring to life the experiences of a boy and his family and friends in ancient times, many of the happenings and the people in this story are fiction.

The *halachos* have been checked and re-checked for accuracy. You will find their sources in the footnotes and can look them up yourself. Because, to our sorrow, today we don't have the Beis HaMikdash, some of the *halachos* mentioned in the book are applied differently in our times. Therefore, no ruling in this book should be seen as a definitive *p'sak*.

The numbers in parentheses in the text correspond to the charts and maps that are included throughout the book. In this way, you will be able to see for yourself where the different structures and objects in the Beis HaMikdash were situated.

It is our hope that young readers will benefit greatly from having a glimpse of our glorious past, and life in the Holy Land when the Beis HaMikdash stood. May it be rebuilt speedily in our days, Amen.

The BeChatzros Beis Hashem Institute

THE BECHATZROS BEIS HASHEM INSTITUTE'S goal is to acquaint young readers with the laws concerning the Beis HaMikdash and the Divine Service in an innovative way that will capture and thrill their hearts and minds. We sincerely hope to be among the privileged to see the Beis HaMikdash rebuilt speedily in our days, and to witness the Divine Service being carried out by the Kohanim.

Our aim is to make it easier and more interesting for children and youth to learn the *halachos* connected with the Beis HaMikdash, and thus attract them to the concepts discussed in the relevant *masechtos* and encourage them to study these texts in detail.

We humbly thank Hashem for blessing our books with great success. They have been enthusiastically welcomed and accepted in all religious circles, and appear in Hebrew, English, Yiddish, and Spanish.

Our first book, *Three Special Days*, describes the *aliyah le-regel* for the Festival of Pesach and the beauty of experiencing a Pesach Seder in the shadow of the Beis HaMikdash, along with the *halachos* of *korban Pesach*.

Seven Special Weeks, our second book, presents a concise anthology of the *halachos* discussed in *Masechtos Middos, Zevachim* and *Tamid*, interwoven with the laws of purification of a *metzora* and the burning of the *Parah Adumah*. A parallel storyline describes an insidious plot launched by the Tzedokim.

The third volume in this series, *One Special Prayer*, deals with the Yom Kippur *avodah* as well as the activities of the Kohen Gadol in the week leading up to the holy day. The sending of the goat *LaAzazel* is also described in detail. Everything is woven together with an exciting intrigue involving treacherous Kohanim and disaffected Tzedokim who conspire to depose the Kohen Gadol and disrupt the Yom Kippur service.

The King's Special Loaves, the fourth book, depicted the thrilling atmosphere of Shavuos in the Beis HaMikdash, while giving a taste of a multitude of topics covered in *Maseches Menachos*. All this occurs with the looming question of whether the Roman army will conquer Yerushalayim on its way to Turkey and loot the Beis HaMikdash.

In *Special Days of Joy*, the fifth in the series, the reader is transported back in time to the Festival of Sukkos in the Beis HaMikdash. The excitement of *Hakhel, nisuch ha-mayim*, and the *Simchas Beis HaSho'eivah* are all highlighted, along with *halachos* of *tum'ah* and the *avodah* of the holiday. Interwoven throughout is a suspenseful tale concerning the mystery of four precious goblets and a long-lost tune, leading up to a thrilling, surprise ending.

Eight Special Nights is the sixth volume in the series. It is set earlier than the other volumes, during the reign of the evil King Antiochus. The stirring story of Chanukah — the rallying of the Chashmonaim, the miraculous defeat of the Greek army, and the miracle of the Menorah lights — combines with a cliffhanging narrative of true *mesirus nefesh*. As a class of young boys hides in a cave with their Rebbi, they learn the laws of *kiddush HaShem* and *kiddush ha-chodesh*, and the structure of the compartments of the *Heichal* — and are almost captured! Through plots and counterplots, treachery and kindness, the riveting saga leads to the emotional liberation of Yerushalayim and the renewal of the *avodah* in the Beis HaMikdash.

Chapter One

In the Middle of the Night

The small candle flickered for another minute and then went out. The twelve-year-old boy who was lying on his right side turned over onto his left, trying to find a more comfortable position. Maybe, finally, he would get some much-needed sleep. But it was no use. As much as he padded his mattress with bundles of straw, he could still feel the hard ground of the cave underneath him.

Sleep was still far from coming, and the further it was, the more he longed for home. Naftali missed his family terribly, and he constantly worried about their welfare.

"Abba, Ima, my little Yeshayahu! Are you okay? What's happening to you in Yerushalayim, now that the city has been conquered?"

He blinked his eyes, trying to stop the tears. In his mind, he could hear the words of his *rebbi* echoing. "Our nation has weathered many difficult times!" he had told his students passionately one day. "Even in the most challenging of times, Hashem did not abandon us. Our forefathers were slaves in Egypt. For years they were cruelly forced to perform the worst slave labor, but they never stopped believing in Hashem and in His promise: 'Hashem will surely remember you and take you up out of this land.'[1] They

---

1. *Bereishis* 50:24.

1

had every reason in the world to despair, but they never stopped hoping and waiting for a better future. In the end, they were redeemed 'with a mighty hand and with an outstretched arm and with great awe and with signs and wonders.'"[2]

With a loving glance at his students, the *rebbi* had added, "The *pasuk* says, 'Hashem will not abandon His nation and He will not leave His portion.'[3] We may not give up, children! With our faith in Hashem, we will merit to see His salvation soon!"

The two candles that were still lit inside the cave did little to bolster his spirits.

"I know that what my *rebbi* said is true. But it's so hard! How can I have faith when everything around me is so dark and gloomy, without a glimmer of hope?" Naftali sat up in distress. He listened to the peaceful, even breathing of his sleeping friends.

"How can you sleep?" His entire being silently screamed the question. "Don't you know what's going on outside?!"

"Rebbi, wake up," he pleaded wordlessly. "I feel like I'm about to collapse. I need someone to help me, to give me the strength to go on!"

Naftali bit his lip hard, trying to choke back the sobs that threatened to burst forth. "For this our heart has become ill, for these things our eyes have grown dim..."[4] He whispered the *pasuk* one word at a time, rocking back and forth in agony. How perfectly Yirmeyahu's[5] prophetic words in *Megillas Eichah* captured their situation now. The image of the desecrated Beis HaMikdash filled his mind's eye and made it difficult for him to breathe.

---

2. *Devarim* 26:8.
3. *Tehillim* 94:14.
4. *Eichah* 5:17.
5. *Bava Basra* 15a; Rashi, *Eichah* 1:1.

"How can you sleep?" His entire being silently screamed the question.

"Such darkness has enveloped us since the Greeks came to power! Greece, the kingdom of darkness, has darkened the eyes of Bnei Yisrael![6] The wicked Greeks stroll fearlessly through the Beis HaMikdash. 'For Har Tzion that is desolate; foxes walk on it.'"[7]

Tears drenched his face, and a sob escaped his throat. "For this our heart has become ill."

Just a few years ago, everything was so wonderful! The pictures flashed through his mind, each one making him cry harder. The *Azarah* on Yom Kippur, snow white from the mass of people bowing down together. The happiness shining on people's faces during the *Simchas Beis HaSho'eivah*. The tumult in the streets of Yerushalayim when it was time to bring *bikkurim*. "How long will You smolder at Your people's prayer?" the words of the *pasuk* cried out. "You have fed them the bread of tears, and You made them drink abundant tears. You set us in conflict with our neighbors, and our enemies scoff among themselves." [8]

A suspicious rustle to his left startled him, and he held his breath. His whole body was on alert.

"Naftali, you're not sleeping?" At the sound of the drowsy voice, he was flooded with relief.

"Reuven, you scared me! I thought they were coming to take us away!" Now that he had a listening ear, all his thoughts came tumbling out. "How much longer can things go on like this? I can't anymore!" He burst out crying again. "I'm worried about my family. The Greeks are after us. We're not allowed to keep Shabbos or learn Torah in public.[9] The Beis HaMikdash is locked up — or rather I wish it was locked up! Our Beis HaMikdash is

---

6. *Yalkut Shimoni, Bereishis* 76.

7. *Eichah* 5:18.

8. *Tehillim* 80:5–7.

9. Rambam, *Hilchos Chanukah* 3:1.

wide open and those *resha'im* are desecrating it! They sacrifice offerings to their idols on our pure, holy *Mizbeach*!"[10]

He couldn't continue talking. In the dark, he felt his friend reach out and grasp his hand. Reuven was breathing heavily now, on the verge of tears himself.

"What do you think?" Reuven finally said in a trembling voice. "I'm not worried? I don't miss home? Who knows where my father is and what's happening to him. Is he still alive? Or maybe… Since the Greeks caught him and sold him as a slave we haven't had any sign of life from him. But even so, we cannot despair!" he said with feeling.

"Remember what happened over two hundred years ago," he continued in a softer tone. "The Jewish people were in danger of annihilation. Achashveirosh, the king of Persia, decreed destruction upon us. He instructed his people to kill all the Jews on the thirteenth of Adar. It seemed like all was lost, when suddenly, salvation came in the most amazing way.

"Soon, Naftali, soon. Now, when everything looks so bleak without even a sliver of light in the world, now is when the salvation will spring up. Hashem can do anything! He can save us at this very moment! We must continue to trust in Him, Naftali. Just trust in Him."

*   *   *

This conversation took place in a spacious, well-hidden cave along the side of one of the mountains surrounding Yerushalayim, during the time of the Second Beis HaMikdash. The Second Beis HaMikdash had been built two hundred and ten years earlier, after the Persians, who ruled the world at the time, approved its construction. Thirty-four years after it was built, the Greeks

---

10. Mishnah *Middos* 1:6.

conquered the Persians, and as part of their military campaign, they invaded Eretz Yisrael as well.[11]

As the Greek empire flourished, hard times fell upon the Jews, times that are etched in blood in the history of our people.

The holy Torah is compared to light, as it says, "Because a mitzvah is a lamp and the Torah is light."[12] Chazal teach that the *pasuk*, "...and darkness on the face of the depths,"[13] is a reference to the kingdom of Greece.[14] From the time Greece took over the world, a fierce spiritual battle erupted between light and darkness. On one side stood the Greeks, trying with all their might to convince the world to worship their idols and to erase our belief in Hashem. On the other side, staunch and faithful, were the Jews who were loyal to Hashem and his Torah, and who wished to keep His mitzvos.

The Greeks left the Beis HaMikdash standing, but they made many terrible decrees to wage war against us both physically and spiritually. Not all the Jews withstood the tremendous pressure. Some of them preferred to act like the Greeks and become *misyavnim*, to spare themselves from persecution and a life of fear. The first to be *misyavein* were the Tzedokim and the Baitosim, who only believed in the Written Torah and did not keep the Oral Torah and the decrees of the Sages.[15] These Jews, whose *emunah* was weak to begin with, were the first to leave the path of Torah.

The Greeks did not give up. When they saw that there were some Jews who still kept mitzvos in secret, they intensified the

---

11. *Avodah Zarah* 9a.

12. *Mishlei* 6:23.

13. *Bereishis* 1:2.

14. *Bereishis Rabbah* 2:4.

15. Rambam, *Peirush HaMishnayos, Avos* 1:3.

decrees. A year before our story takes place, the Greeks captured Har HaBayis. They locked all the *batei midrash* and *batei knesses* in Yerushalayim and erected altars for idol worship in every corner of the city. And if that wasn't enough, they dared to offer up a pig on the *Mizbeach*!

Jews who were caught doing mitzvos were brutally slaughtered. The atmosphere in the Jewish neighborhoods was tense and gloomy.

*   *   *

The ceramic cups on the table clinked loudly against each other.

"We must do something to save the Torah!" Elkanah the Levi practically shouted, thumping his hand hard on the table for emphasis.

"Watch out! You're breaking the cups," his brother Yochanan pointed out.

"Yochanan, I'm talking to you about the future of our nation, and you're worried about ceramic cups?! The *batei midrash* are closed; where will the children learn?!"

"I'm just grasping on to the firm hope that Hashem will not abandon us," said Yochanan, moving the cups to the middle of the table, out of harm's way. "I'm sure that soon we will see His salvation. My *rebbi* told me that he learned from his teachers that every rung on Yaakov's ladder represents one full year. In his dream, Yaakov Avinu saw the ministering angels of the nations going up and then coming down. The angel of Bavel went up seventy rings, and indeed, we were exiled to Bavel for seventy years. The angel of Persia went up fifty-two rungs before he descended; those were the fifty-two years of Persian rule. The angel of Greece went up one hundred and eighty rungs.[16] Based

---

16. *Vayikra Rabbah* 29:2.

on that, we can figure that that Greek rule will come to an end soon."

"I am jealous of your tranquility in the face of such persecution," Elkanah said candidly. "I so wish that this evil rule will come to an end already! But how do you know from when to start calculating the one hundred and eighty years? Besides, there's no loss like lost time.[17] Even if we do merit to be saved in a few more weeks, every day that goes by without the children learning Torah is an irreplaceable loss."

He rested his head in his hands and let out a heavy sigh. His brother laid a hand on his shoulder.

"You are so right, Elkanah. Let's not forget that the Torah is our best defense against the *yetzer hara*.[18] The *yetzer hara* is running wild in the streets right now. The Greeks are persuading our youth to abandon what is truly important and instead to put all their energy into sports and body building. If we don't strengthen the youth with Torah, how will they withstand the temptations of the *yetzer hara*?"

This penetrating question hung in the air for a long moment. Elkanah was silent, and Yochanan paced back and forth along the length of the room, trying to find a solution.

"I may have an idea," Elkanah finally said. "But I'll need your help. Do you remember the cave we found when we were young boys hiking outside Yerushalayim?"

"Of course!" A nostalgic smile spread across Yochanan's face. "It was a big cave with a narrow, hidden opening, about a two-hour walk from Yerushalayim. There was even a small, clear spring bubbling inside the cave."

"That's the one. I went there recently, and the cave looks just

---

17. *Midrash Shmuel* on *Avos* 5:21.
18. *Kiddushin* 30b.

as it did then. In fact, for our purposes, it's even better than it used to be. Thick brush now blocks the entrance to the cave, making it an excellent hiding place. It took me almost two hours to find the entrance."

Understanding dawned in Yochanan's eyes.

"I want to take a group of eleven- and twelve-year-old boys and learn Torah with them," Elkanah continued. "We'll stay in the cave until the danger has passed. Of course, there is some risk involved, but there is a very good chance that no one will find us."

"May Hashem be with you, Elkanah! But what's my part in the whole plan?"

Elkanah fixed him with a determined stare.

"You are going to be responsible for providing us with food and other necessities. There's plenty of water there, and there's even a small pool that we can immerse in. While you arrange everything else that we need, I'll try to get a group of boys together.

"I'll have to find the right sort of boys — strong-willed and brave. I'll also have to convince their parents. They'll have to agree to part from their children for a long time. The boys won't be allowed to walk around outside and risk giving away our hiding place."

Elkanah's mission turned out to be easier than he expected. Parents sent their children willingly, and their dedication to Torah lifted his spirits.

In the meantime, Yochanan equipped the cave to the best of his abilities. He set up a sleeping area padded with straw mattresses and a study corner with hewn stones for seating. There was even a wooden cupboard that held a small *sefer Torah* and the books of the *Nevi'im*. In another corner, he piled up mounds of figs, apples, and other foods that do not spoil easily, as well as a large quantity of candles and two lanterns.

Within a week, everything was ready and twelve boys were transferred to the cave in small groups. Already on the first day, the sounds of Torah learning echoed through the cave nonstop, just as Elkanah had hoped.

As agreed, Yochanan came twice a week to deliver provisions and letters from home.

Chapter Two

Matters of Life and Death

A basket loaded with figs stood in the center of the table. The boys sat around in a circle, listening intently to their *rebbi*.

"Let's imagine the following scene: A Jew walks down the street, when suddenly a Greek leaps out and grabs him and orders him to transgress one of the mitzvos in the Torah or be killed on the spot. Should he give up his life or transgress and save himself?"

Elkanah looked at the boys and waited.

Naftali, the sharpest thinker of the bunch, was the first to respond. "It says, 'You shall observe My statutes and My laws, which a man shall do and live by them.'[1] From here, the *Chachamim* learn, 'Live by them, and not to die by them.'[2] Based on this *pasuk*, it's better to do an *aveirah* than to die."

"When it comes to Shabbos, the halachah is that even if we're not sure that a person's life is in danger, we desecrate Shabbos in order to save him,"[3] agreed Mahalalel, a short boy with bright eyes. "And that's for Shabbos, which is such a holy day! Keeping

---

1. *Vayikra* 18:5.
2. *Sanhedrin* 74a.
3. *Yoma* 83a.

Shabbos is equivalent to all the other mitzvos[4] and one who des-
ecrates it gets the worst death penalty — he is stoned!"[5]

At that, Shimshon jumped up from his seat. "If so, then why
did Avraham Avinu prefer to be burned in a fiery furnace than to
worship idols?"[6]

"Maybe he wanted to be extra strict, so he was willing to give
up his life even though he was really allowed to sin and not be
killed," suggested Mahalalel uncertainly.

"Impossible!" cried tall, skinny Zechariah. "How could he
choose to be strict when the *pasuk* clearly says, '*vachai bahem* —
live by them'?"

Elkanah quietly followed the debate, a satisfied smile on his
face.

"Well, Avraham lived before the Torah was given," piped up
a small, hesitant voice.

"But the *Avos* kept the entire Torah!" two other boys chorused
in response.

Elkanah raised his hand for quiet.

"I'm happy that you're so enthusiastic," he said, "but we must
remember to speak quietly so the sound of our voices does not
reach unwelcome ears, *chas v'chalilah*. We mustn't forget that the
walls have ears."[7]

"Rebbi, is it true that the *Avos* kept the whole Torah?" asked
Reuven quietly.

"Absolutely," confirmed Elkanah. "The Sages teach that Avraham
Avinu kept even mitzvos *d'Rabbanan*, such as *eiruv tavshilin*."[8]

---

4. *Shemos Rabbah* 25:12.

5. *Sanhedrin* 53a.

6. *Bereishis Rabbah* 38:13.

7. Rashi, *Berachos* 8b, s.v. *ela ba'sadeh*.

8. *Yoma* 28b.

"Well, then, why didn't Avraham keep the halachah of *'vachai bahem'*?" countered Naftali, who was nicknamed "Swift" Naftali, because he was quick as a deer, like his Biblical namesake.

"Maybe the halachah is different when it comes to *avodah zarah*. That's one of the most important ideas in the Torah!" answered Zevulun.

The babble of voices died down slowly. The boys turned their eyes to their *rebbi*, waiting for him to resolve all the questions and contradictions. This discussion was particularly close to their hearts, because it was not a theoretical question. It was one that came up on a daily basis since the Greeks had begun trying to lure them away from their religion.

Elkanah placed a loving hand on the child next to him, and said softly, "The halachah of *'ya'avor v'al yeihareig,'* he should transgress rather than be killed, applies to almost every one of the 613 mitzvos.[9] That means that if a Jew has the choice to sin or be killed, he should do the sin and not allow himself to be killed. However, there are three mitzvos about which we say *'yeihareig v'al ya'avor,'* he should be killed rather than transgress. These three mitzvos are *avodah zarah* — idol worship; *giluy arayos* — immorality; and *shfichus damim* — murder."

"Why is the halachah different for these three mitzvos?" three children asked in unison.

"Just this morning, we said *'Shema Yisrael Hashem Elokeinu Hashem Echad'* with *kavanah*, and then we said, *'V'ahavta eis Hashem Elokecha b'chol l'vavecha u'v'chol nafshecha…'*[10] Chazal explain that the words *u'v'chol nafshecha*, with all your soul, mean 'even if they are taking your life.'[11] A Jew is obligated to give up his life and

---

9. *Sanhedrin* 74a.

10. *Devarim* 6:4–5.

11. *Berachos* 54a.

not worships other gods, because idol worship contradicts our core belief that there is One God and no other besides Him."[12]

The *rebbi* leaned forward as he spoke, deep creases lining his forehead. This was a fundamental, essential topic, and he wanted to teach it to the children in the clearest way possible.

"And why must we give up our lives to avoid transgressing the prohibitions of *shfichus damim* and *giluy arayos*?"

A slight smile played across Elkanah's lips. His clever students wouldn't leave him be until they fully understood the subject.

"When it comes to *shfichus damim*, we learn out this halachah not from a *pasuk*, but from logical deduction. Think for a minute; maybe you can figure out the logic yourselves. But please, remember to speak quietly!"

The children scrunched up their faces in concentration. Reuven drummed his fingers on the ground, which helped him focus. Boaz, the youngest of the group, surprised everyone by speaking up first.

"Well, it's sort of obvious," he said, spreading out his palms. "If a Gentile comes and tells a Jew to kill another Jew or be killed, of course he has no right to kill that other Jew. The Torah that tells us '*vachai bahem*' prefers that a mitzvah be transgressed so that the life of a Jew will be preserved; but in this case, where one Jew will die no matter what, there is no reason to transgress the prohibition of *shfichus damim*, and it is better to be killed than to do this *aveirah*."[13]

"Wonderful! Wonderful!" said the *rebbi* with obvious pleasure. "Boaz, you've made me so happy with your excellent thinking!"

It was moments like these that gave Elkanah the strength to

---

12. *Sanhedrin* 74a.

13. Rashi, ibid., s.v. *sevara*.

continue. His work with the children was not easy. They were so young, and already they were away from home and exposed to great suffering. He had to be so patient with them, encouraging them and bolstering their spirits regularly. But moments like this made it all worth it.

"What about *giluy arayos*?" The boys, eager to know more, wouldn't let him get lost in thought for too long.

"Here, the halachah is learned from a *pasuk* that equates *shfichus damim* and *giluy arayos*. 'Because as when a man rises up against his fellow and murders him, so too is this thing.'[14] The same way the rule of *yeihareig v'al ya'avor* applies to *shfichus damim*, it applies to *giluy arayos*."[15]

"There's something I don't understand." Zevulun, a boy with coal-black eyes, stood up from his place on the hard ground and fixed his *rebbi* with questioning look. "Why did my uncle refuse to listen to his Greek neighbor who insisted that he desecrate Shabbos? Was he supposed to desecrate Shabbos and not die? Was it a sin that my uncle refused to listen to that Greek and gave up his life?"

"When did all this happen, Zevulun?" Elkanah, who could read between the lines, understood that this child desperately needed to speak about the event, which had clearly made a very deep impression on me.

Zevulun bit his lip and wiped away tears that began to form in his eyes.

"It was about a year ago," he said in a low voice, eyes on the ground in front of him. "My relatives were at home, eating their Shabbos meal, singing beautiful *zemiros* between each course. It seems that they got carried away with their heartfelt singing and

---

14. *Devarim* 22:26.
15. *Sanhedrin* 74a.

raised their voices a bit too much. The echoes of their songs were heard by the hotheaded Greek who lived in the house next door. Suddenly, in the middle of their meal, the door burst open. The Greek neighbor stood there, brandishing a long sword.

"'Stop your singing right this minute!' he roared at my uncle. 'Light a fire, or I'll kill you with this sword!'

"My aunt told us that my uncle remained calm and composed. Everyone else froze in terror, but he didn't flinch.

""'Do whatever you wish to me, but I will not desecrate the Shabbos!' he said quietly but firmly.

Zevulun's voice dropped until it was barely audible.

"The Greek lunged at him in fury and stabbed him with his sword in front of his wife and children."

"Your uncle acted according to halachah, and how fortunate he is to have such a great *zechus*!" said Elkanah. "He merited a distinguished place in Gan Eden and no creature can stand in his in his place, because he was killed *al kiddush HaShem*.[16] I'll explain to you why he was right to give up his life, even though it was not for one of the three severe *aveiros* that we listed before. Listen carefully."

The boys tensed up. Some of them leaned forward and others moved up a little closer so they wouldn't miss a single word.

"Let's say, for example," Elkanah said slowly, trying to find a good example, "a non-Jew tells a Jew to cook food for him on Shabbos because he's hungry. In this case, the rule of '*vachai bahem*' applies, and he must desecrate Shabbos and not let him himself be killed.[17]

"However, in a case where the non-Jew tells a Jew to sin not for his own personal benefit but solely to get him to sin, if there

---

16. *Bava Basra* 10b.
17. *Sanhedrin* 74b.

are ten Jews present, the Jew must sacrifice his life, and by doing so he fulfills the mitzvah[18] of 'I will become holy among Bnei Yisrael.'"[19]

"That's exactly what happened to Zevulun's uncle!" Mahalalel burst out, cutting into the *rebbi*'s words. "But one minute, were there ten Jews there?"

"I don't think so," Zevulun said quietly.

"I'm not finished yet," said Elkanah, a gentle hint to Mahalel that he shouldn't have interrupted. "There are times when even if a person is all alone, he is required to give up his life. When is that? During times of *shmad*, when the Gentiles make decrees against the Jewish religion, to try and get the Jews to become just like them.[20]

"Unfortunately, we are facing very difficult times. The Greeks want to stop us from doing mitzvos. In times like these, even if a person is alone he must be killed rather than transgress a single one of the mitzvos of the Torah, just as Zevulun's righteous uncle did.

"Did you know, children? During times of *shmad*, a Jew must give up his life not just for something like Shabbos, which is one our most important mitzvos. He also must give up his life for more minor mitzvos, and even for Jewish customs! For example, we Jews tie our shoes a certain way. If a Gentile tries to force us to tie our shoes the way the Gentiles do, we must be killed rather than do so."[21]

*   *   *

---

18. Rambam, *Hilchos Yesodei HaTorah* 5:1.

19. *Vayikra* 22:32.

20. *Sanhedrin* 74a.

21. Ibid., 74b.

In the holy city of Yerushalayim, in the home of the Sages of the Sanhedrin, a heated debate was taking place.

The windows were shuttered and the curtains closed. Those present sat in an inner room, and spoke in hushed voices.

"We can't continue this way!" whispered a fervent young *dayan*, rising from his seat. "We must revolt against the evil kingdom of Greece!"

"But we don't stand a chance against them!" replied another *dayan* miserably. "They are stronger than us and they outnumber us by far. If that weren't enough, many Jews have already adopted a Greek lifestyle and become just like the Greeks. Surely they'll object to a revolt."

"We must at least try!" cried the first *dayan*, and immediately lowered his voice. "How can we just stand by when the entire future of the Jewish people is at stake?"

"But if we get up and fight, the Greeks will immediately mobilize their army and quash the revolt effortlessly!"

A heavy silence hung in the room. The *dayanim* looked hopeless.

Then one of the most important *dayanim* clapped his hands together in consternation. "What's come over us all? Have we forgotten that Hashem can save us, no matter how many or how few we number? With only twelve thousand men, Pinchas defeated the Midianite army,[22] and not a single Jew was harmed![23]

"A little later in history, Gid'on fought the Midianites with just three hundred men.[24] And what about young Dovid? Armed with a slingshot and five stones he faced Golias, the Pelishti giant, and

---

22. *Bemidbar* 31:5.

23. Ibid., 31:49.

24. *Shoftim* 7.

killed him![25] The danger of *shmad* is hovering over us! Let's stand up and fight and Hashem will help us!"

His passionate words made a deep impression on everyone present, but then another *dayan*, who hadn't uttered a word until now, spoke up.

"The question is if according to halachah we are allowed to revolt against the Greeks, because we would be putting ourselves at risk of annihilation, *chas v'chalilah*. In the days of Mordechai and Esther, even though there were decrees of destruction and *shmad* against the Jews, the Jews did not revolt. They fasted and davened until Hashem saved them."

"Of course we have to daven," agreed a distinguished-looking sage. "But how long can we allow the Greeks to do whatever they please? We've been under their terrible rule for over a hundred years, and the decrees are getting worse. With no shame whatsoever, they entered the holiest of places and defiled it! How can we not protest?"

"The fact is that Mordechai waited for the decree to be cancelled and avoided a conflict."

"You can't compare the two cases," an elderly sage stated unequivocally. "Let's not forget that during Mordechai's times, the wicked Haman was hanged just a few days after the decree was passed. It could very well be that if salvation hadn't come so soon, the Jews would have revolted against the Persians. Moreover, the Persians planned to kill the Jews and harm their bodies, while the Greeks are trying to destroy our spirits and force us to assimilate![26] They want to distance us from HaKadosh Baruch Hu. How can we remain silent when Hashem's Name is being disgraced?!"

Quiet descended on the room once again. This was not a

---

25. *I Shmuel* 17.
26. Rav Elchonon Wasserman, *Kovetz Ma'amarim*, p. 94.

simple decision. The responsibility weighed heavily on the Sages' shoulders and they were terribly afraid that the wrong decision would have consequences too horrible to imagine.

*   *   *

"*Chas v'chalilah*, it shouldn't happen, but what will we do if the Greeks discover us and order us to bow down to an idol?" Elkanah's face was serious as he waited for an answer from his students.

"We will die *al kiddush HaShem*!" was the boys' unanimous answer, delivered in a babble of voices. "We will sanctify Hashem's Name!"

Chapter Three

Thirty-Eight Compartments

At the Ministry of Education, a sense of failure pervaded the atmosphere. Sperkus, the chief minister, had invested enormous effort in an attempt to give Jewish children a Greek education. He developed a curriculum and instituted it in all the schools, under the title "Innovative Education."

"If there are no kids there are no goats," he would repeat day and night. "Everything starts from the youth! If the young people are with us, the Jewish nation has no future!" he preached.

But despite his best efforts and the huge sums of money he sank into the new educational program, the religious children still were not on board. In fact, many of Yerushalayim's children simply seemed to vanish.

True, the schools weren't empty; the classes were full of children whose enthusiastic parents had sent them there to learn. But those were Tzedoki children. Among the children of the Perushim, there were just a few hundred children who came to school every day against their will and sat stock-still in class, as if oblivious to everything they saw or heard there.

A careful investigation by the Ministry of Education revealed that these children's parents learned Torah with them every night in order to combat the harmful influence of the Greek teachers.

Determined to succeed, Sperkus sent the Greek police, who were responsible for enforcing mandatory education laws, to snoop around in these homes and stop them. Though they did catch a child or two here or there, according to their lists there were thousands of missing children who had disappeared from the scene, gone without a trace.

Sperkus would not give up. He launched a series of inquiries, surveillances, and secret spy missions to uncover as much information as he could. His findings indicated that many parents had sent their children to villages throughout Eretz Yisrael. In these small towns there was little or no supervision over the educational system and they could study Torah without fear.

Rumor on the street had it that Torah was also being studied in secret, in basements located under city homes. Furious and resolute, Sperkus sent inspectors from the Ministry accompanied by police to comb the houses thoroughly and carry out surprise raids.

"We must catch at least one group," he explained to his men. "I'm sure that after we catch one group of children and punish them severely, many more parents will begin sending their children to our enlightened, progressive schools," he said, oblivious to the fact that Greece's hard-fisted methods were the very opposite of "enlightenment" and "progress."

A tip-off from a Tzedoki neighbor brought Greek forces to a home in a small alleyway in Yerushalayim, where a group of children was purported to gather every night. The soldiers looked through the window, staring dumbfounded at the children playing happily. The few bookshelves in the room contained only works of Greek philosophy and no Jewish books at all.

Sperkus, who received a report of the incident a little while layer, paced back and forth in his office like a caged lion. He called for his secretary and instructed him to write up the details of the situation and send the information to the Greek ruler in Eretz Yisrael.

The soldiers looked through the window,
staring dumbfounded at the children playing happily.

"I did my part," he said, and headed for the gambling hall that had been erected on the outskirts of Yerushalayim.

The ruler read the report and his face darkened. Without hesitating, he sent a letter to the Greek police chief in Yerushalayim, which contained a subtle reprimand along with a demand that he do his best to assist the Ministry of Education.

Pelagios, the Greek chief of police, was irate. "What do I feed you and pay you for, anyway?" he roared at his officers. "Tens of thousands of little children are learning Torah in secret, and you, big heroes that you are, can't even catch one of them! The only thing that interests you is fine wine and grilled meat! All you want is food and fun!" His voice rose higher and higher, and the officers cowered in fear. "Within a month, I want the number of children in our schools to double. And if not, heads will roll! You are hereby warned!"

*   *   *

Winter was rapidly approaching, bringing new hardships to the cave-dwelling children.

In the summer months, the boys had enjoyed the cool climate in the cave, but now cold winds blew in and sleeping on the frigid ground was extremely unpleasant.

On Yochanan's next visit, he and Elkanah held an emergency consultation.

"Winter is on its way, and the children are already suffering," Elkanah said. "They learned so well the whole summer, but we can't continue in these conditions. We must find a solution. There has to be some way to heat this place."

"Maybe we can burn wood at the edge of the cave? The fire will warm things up," Yochanan suggested.

"Not an option," replied his brother. "The whole cave will fill with smoke and we won't be able to breathe."

Yochanan rapped on the wall of the cave. "We'll dig a chimney," he said simply.

"But then the smoke will go out the chimney and everyone will see it! It'll give away our hiding place," Elkanah shook his head in the negative.

"What if you only heat the wood at night? Then no one will notice the smoke. This area is completely deserted at night."

"Hmm, that sounds better already," agreed Elkanah. "Let's try it and see."

Yochanan didn't waste any time. The next day he arrived at the cave accompanied by two friends and laden with supplies: warm clothes, thick woolen blankets and digging tools.

After briefly surveying the cave, they chose a corner off to the side where the heat would spread throughout the whole cave, and they began to dig a narrow shaft that was fifty feet long. The crew made careful calculations in order to direct the opening to a place where it would be concealed by thick brush.

When they finished reinforcing the chimney walls by various means, they set out into forest and spent an entire day cutting branches and chopping wood, which they then piled up in one of the "rooms" of the cave.

*   *   *

The boys' school day was carefully planned to include everything they needed to learn: *Chumash*, *Navi* and practical halachah, such as the laws of *berachos*, Shabbos, *kashrus*, *ribbis*, and the four types of *shomrim* (people who are responsible for watching someone else's property). Elkanah knew he was educating the next generation of *talmidei chachamim* and he carried out his role with the utmost seriousness and dedication, teaching every subject clearly and thoroughly.

A once-a-week lesson focused on the structure of the Beis HaMikdash and the *korbanos*. During their free time, Reuven and Yehudah built a miniature model of the Beis HaMikdash. With golden hands and endless patience, they carved out wooden walls with a pocket knife and attached them together with glue that they made from flour and water. Every day, they sat hunched over their project, adding more items and additional details. So far, they had built the *Ulam*(10), the *Heichal*(11) and the *Kodesh Ha-Kodashim*(12). In the *Heichal*, they had placed a tiny *Shulchan*(85), *Menorah*(84), and *Mizbeach HaZahav*(83). Between the *Heichal* and the *Kodesh HaKodashim* they hung two *parochos*(19) that they cut from small scraps of fabric.

Their friends watched their progress with mixed feelings. The miniature building reminded them how much they missed that holy place that was so precious to them. At the same time, their hearts filled with pain when they thought about how the Beis HaMikdash was now defiled and disgraced, in the hands of ruthless captors.

*   *   *

With loving hands, Yehudah put the model on the table that everyone was sitting at.

"I think that our little builders will have a lot of work to do this week," said their *rebbi*, winking at them affectionately. "At the moment, the model has only three rooms: the *Ulam*(10), the *Heichal*(11) and the *Kodesh HaKodashim*(12). Today, I'm going to tell you about another thirty-eight rooms(69)."

"We'll have to make our Beis HaMikdash ten times bigger! It'll take up the whole table!" Yehudah remarked enthusiastically.

The *rebbi* smiled, placing a gentle hand on top of the model. "They're small rooms that don't take up very much space," he said. "These thirty-eight rooms, which are called *ta'im*, compartments(69), surround the *Heichal* and the *Kodesh HaKodashim* on three sides: north, south and west."[1]

"And on the east?" Zevulun couldn't resist asking, even though

---

1. Mishnah *Middos* 4:3.

The Ulam (Antechamber),
Heichal (Temple Chamber),
and Kodesh HaKodashim (Holy of Holies)

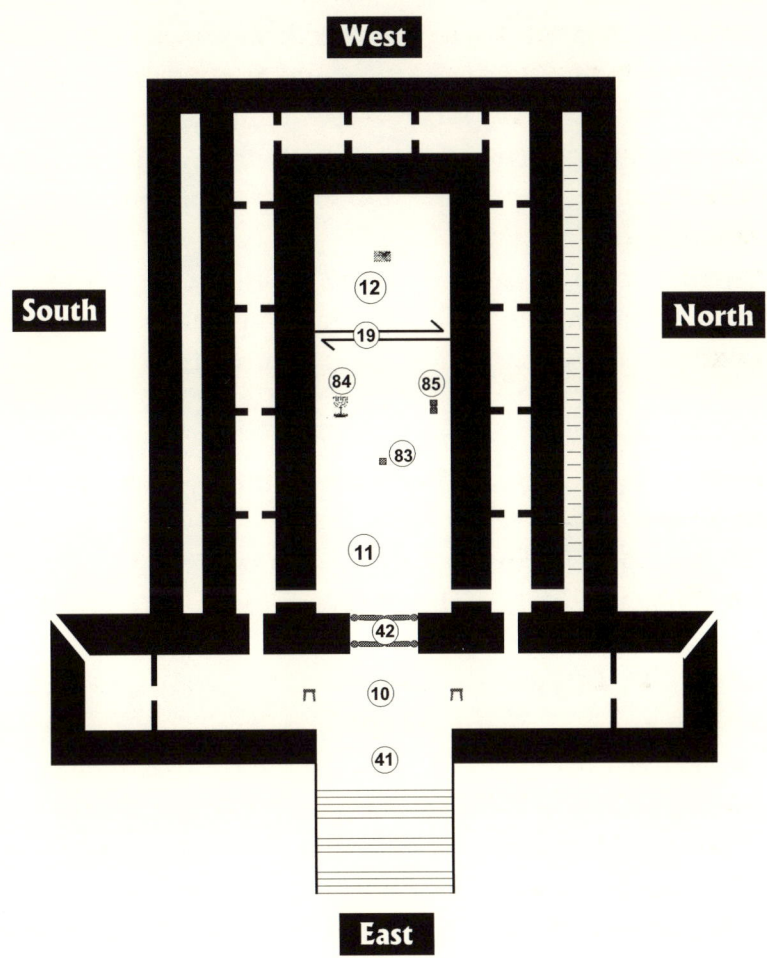

10. *Ulam*
11. *Heichal*
12. *Kodesh HaKodashim*
19. *Amah Teraksin* (two curtains and the passage between them that divided the *Heichal* from the *Kodesh HaKodashim*)

41. Entrance to *Ulam*
42. Entrance to *Heichal*
83. The Golden (Incense) Altar
84. Menorah
85. Showbread Table

he knew that their *rebbi* didn't like questions before he finished his explanation.

"See for yourself," said Elkanah, pointing to the right place. "On the east of the *Heichal*(11) is the *Ulam*(10)."[2] He then continued with his explanation. "There are three levels of compartments, one on top of the other. On the north, there are five compartments on each level, for a total of fifteen compartments. The same thing is found on the south side, as well. All together, on both sides, there are thirty compartments. The remaining eight compartments are on the west side."[3]

"Are they also three levels high?" Shimshon wanted to know.

"Indeed they are. There are three compartments on the lowest level and three on the second level. On the third level there are just two."

Reuven fingered his pocketknife, happily anticipating the work that lay ahead of him, cutting up bits of wood to create the small compartments.

"How high were the compartments?" asked Yehudah, who was already busy calculating the measurements they would use to build their model.

"The *Heichal*(11) is forty *amos* high.[4] Together, the three levels of compartments were lower than the *Heichal*, because the windows of the *Heichal* are located above the compartments.[5]

"Now I understand! When I peered over the Beis HaMikdash through *Sha'ar HaKorban*, the Gate of the Sacrifice(34), I noticed a certain protrusion around the building and I couldn't understand what it was," cried Zechariah, who was the type of person

---

2. Ibid., 4:7.

3. Ibid., 4:3.

4. Ibid., 4:6.

5. *Tiferes Yisrael* on Mishnah *Middos* 4:3, #24.

The Compartments

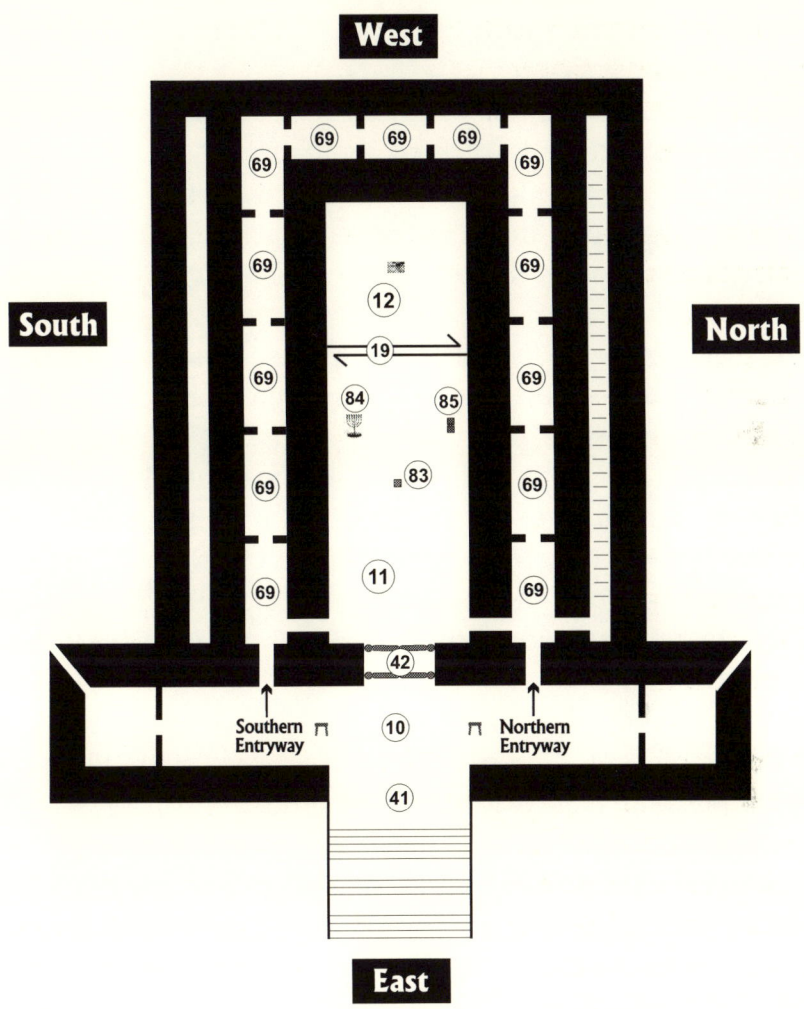

West

South

North

Southern Entryway

Northern Entryway

East

10. *Ulam*
11. *Heichal*
12. *Kodesh HaKodashim*
19. *Amah Teraksin* (two curtains and the passage between them that divided the Heichal from the *Kodesh HaKodashim*)

41. Entrance to *Ulam*
42. Entrance to *Heichal*
69. Compartments
83. The Golden (Incense) Altar
84. Menorah
85. Showbread Table

who noticed details. "Now I know that those were the compart-ments(69) surrounding the *Heichal* and the *Kodesh HaKodashim*."

"Where is the entrance to the compartments?" wondered black-haired Yedidya.

"As we learned, the *Ulam* is wider than the *Heichal*. In the extra space on either side of the *Heichal*, there are two small entryways, called *pishpeshim*, that lead to the compartments; and between one compartment and the next there is a passageway. Practically speaking, even though there are two *pishpeshim*, only the one on the right, north of the *Heichal*, is used for entry.

"The entryway on the left, the southern *pishpesh*, is generally closed. Only Hashem Himself goes through it, and no human be-ing enters it, as the *pasuk* says, 'This gate will be closed, it will not be opened, and no man shall come through it, for Hashem, the God of Yisrael, comes through it, and it will be closed.'[6] This entryway is opened on Shabbos and Rosh Chodesh."

"Who opens it on Shabbos and Rosh Chodesh?" Zevulun never would have guessed what kind of reaction his innocent question would get.

Elkanah's eyes filled with tears and he sighed deeply. "The door opens by itself," he said in a soft voice. "When Shabbos or Rosh Chodesh arrives, the door miraculously turns on its hinges and opens, and when Shabbos is over it closes by itself.[7] That's what the *pasuk* means when it says, 'The gate of the Inner Court that faces toward the east will remain closed the six working days, but on the Shabbos day it will be opened, and on Rosh Chodesh it will be opened.'"[8]

Naftali, always a sensitive soul, was becoming emotional. The

---

6. *Yechezkel* 44:2.

7. *Pirkei D'Rabbi Eliezer* 51.

8. *Yechezkel* 46:1.

The Compartments (Side View)

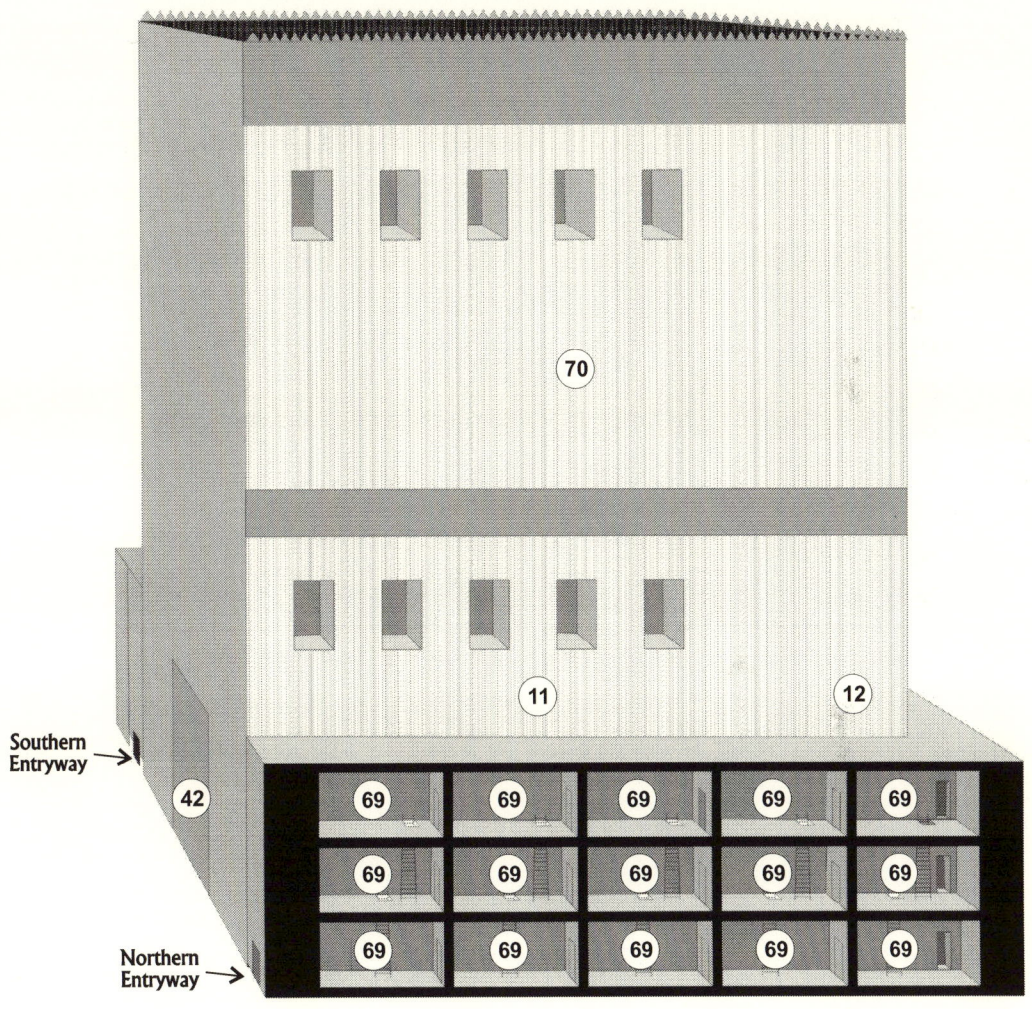

11. *Heichal*
12. *Kodesh HaKodashim*

42. Entrance to *Heichal*
69. Compartments
70. Attic

Beis HaMikdash, the holiest structure in the world, was in impure hands, and idols stood in the *Azarah*. He drew in his breath sharply. On the *Mizbeach* that had offered up thousands and millions of *korbanos* for Hashem, they were now offering sacrifices for *avodah zarah*. What would be in the end? A sob escaped his lips and he covered his face with his hands, letting the tears flow.

"Boys, let's take a break now," Elkanah said, rising from his seat. There was deep understanding in his eyes. "After recess, when you're feeling a bit calmer, we'll continue learning."

Chapter Four

The Missing Miniature

The heart-wrenching sound of Naftali's crying echoed throughout the cave.

Elkanah sat on the side, learning from a parchment scroll and forcibly holding himself back from going over to Naftali.

"Cry, child, cry," he whispered soundlessly. "The pure tears of Jewish children who are free of sin will surely arouse Hashem's mercy."

After a few long minutes, he gently lifted Naftali up and led him to a niche deep inside the cave.

"In Mitzrayim, when it seemed that life was too difficult to bear, that was when the salvation came," whispered Elkanah, keeping his eyes off of Naftali's face.

"But we've been suffering for so long, and we still haven't seen a single ray of light," answered Naftali through his tears. "Maybe we are not worthy of miracles?"

"Do you know," continued the *rebbi* in an attempt to calm the child, "that in Mitzrayim the Jews were deeply involved in sin? They worshipped idols,[1] yet Hashem still searched for merits, so that they could be redeemed. He gave them the mitzvos of *korban Pesach* and *bris milah*; that's what the *pasuk* refers to when it says, 'And I said to you, "With your blood, live," and I said to

---

1. *Yechezkel* 20:5–9.

33

*The guards positioned themselves on a comfortable,
wide branch high up in a leafy tree.*

you, "With your blood, live.""[2] They were saved in the merit of the blood of the *korban Pesach* and the blood of *bris milah*.[3]

"Spiritually, our situation today is far better. There are thousands of Jews who are still loyal to Hashem. With great self-sacrifice, they keep the Torah and are careful about every aspect of halachah, big and small. Hashem can bring the *ge'ulah* in an instant!"

Naftali stood up in a storm of emotion. "Then why? Why? Why doesn't He save us?" His painful cry rang out in the cave. "It's been over six months since I last saw my father and my mother and my adorable little brother Yeshayahu...If we have so many merits, why are we still suffering?"

"I don't know," answered the *rebbi* honestly. "We don't know everything. What I do know is that everything is perfectly calculated by Hashem and is part of His plan. We get exactly the amount of pain and suffering that we are meant to have. HaKadosh Baruch Hu does not remove his special love and providence from us for even a second. He collects every tear that we shed, and rejoices in every mitzvah. *L'fum tzara agra* — when it is more difficult to keep the mitzvos, the reward is that much greater.[4] Every single Jew in our generation who makes the effort to cling to Hashem despite the hardships will receive a reward of unbelievable greatness! You cannot imagine the *nachas* he gives his Father in *Shamayim*!"

*   *   *

During one of the brief nighttime walks that the boys would take to get some fresh air, they discovered a small clearing in the forest five minutes away from the cave. Elkanah was elated by

---

2. Ibid., 16:6.

3. *Rus Rabbah* 6:1.

4. Mishnah *Avos* 5:23.

the discovery, and once a day he allowed the boys to go out to the clearing. There, well hidden by the towering trees all around them, they would have an hour-long lesson.

Despite the danger that this outing entailed, it was necessary for the children's health and the benefits outweighed the risks. Still, Elkanah did not take chances, and he set up a guard-duty rotation among the boys. While the rest of the group was learning, one boy would stand guard on the north side of the clearing and another would stand guard on the south, each one a three-minute walk from the group. The guards positioned themselves on a comfortable, wide branch high up in a leafy tree. That way they could see off into the distance while remaining out of view.

They agreed on a signal that they would give in case of approaching danger: the chirping sound of a cricket indicated that danger was coming from the north, while the call of a coyote meant that trouble was brewing south of the clearing.

The boys sat comfortably on the fresh, low grass that grew in the clearing, gulping in the clear forest air.

"How do you get to the second level of the compartments(69)?" With his question, Zechariah got the day's lesson rolling.

"Every compartment on the lowest level has a ladder that leads to the compartment above it, and there is a ladder going from every second-story compartment to the one above it on the third level.[5] That's in addition to the passageways between one compartment and the next on the same floor," explained the *rebbi*. Reuven looked up at the blue sky that peeked through the branches and thought about how he could build twenty-five miniature ladders.

"That means that some of the compartments had four entrances," Mahalalel was quick to grasp.

---

5. Mishnah *Middos* 4:3.

When he saw his friends' questioning looks, he explained. "I'm talking about the middle compartments on the second floor. They have an entrance on the right and an entrance on the left, another entrance on the bottom of the compartment going to the first floor, and one on the ceiling of the compartment that led to the floor above."

The *rebbi* nodded in approval. "In fact, there is one compartment that has five openings! Let's see if you can figure out which one it was."

The boys thought hard, and for a while the light rustle of the leaves was the only sound.

"Rebbi, tell us, please!" Shimshon finally said.

"It's the first compartment on the north that bordered the wall of the *Ulam*," Elkanah said. "The compartment that you enter to get to all the other compartments"

The boys were very surprised. "That one has five entrances?! According to Rebbi's explanation before, it should only have three!"

"Three?" replied Elkanah, lightly brushing away an ant that was industriously climbing up his cloak. "Can you tell me what they are?"

Reuven spoke up first. "The main entrance from the *Ulam*(10), another entrance to the west to get to the next compartment, and an opening in the ceiling to get to the compartment above."

"Very nice," the rebbi complimented him. "But in addition to those three, there are two more entrances that you still don't know about: one entrance that leads to the *Heichal*(11) and another that goes to the *Mesibah*(23)."

"*Mesibah*? What's that?" asked Yehudah

"Why do you need an opening to the *Heichal*?" Shimon questioned. "There's a nice big entrance to the *Heichal* through the *Ulam*!"[6]

---

6. Ibid., 4:1.

"Slowly, slowly! One thing at a time," Elkanah lifted his hand. "Soon you'll understand everything.

"Let's start with the opening to the *Heichal*. Shimon's question is a valid one. There is an enormous Entrance(42) that allows passage between the *Ulam* and the *Heichal*, but it's locked every night from the inside.[7] In the morning, the Kohanim enter the *Ulam*(10), and then they go through the compartment to get to the *Heichal*(11). Then they unbolt the large doors(42) through which Kohanim will go in and out all day long.

"And now for the *Mesibah*(23). The *Mesibah* is a sloped passageway located in the space between the second and third walls to the north of the *Heichal*."[8]

"North of the *Heichal* there are three parallel walls?" This idea, unfamiliar to the children, took them all by surprise. "We only know about two of them: the wall of the *Heichal* and the outer wall of the compartments, which borders the *Azarah*!"

"So now you'll know something new," answered Elkanah, with a twinkle in his eye. "The outer wall of the compartments does not border the *Azarah*. There are two walls there, with a space in between. Inside this space is the *Mesibah*(23), which is a sloped passageway that leads to the roof of the compartments."[9]

"Is the roof of the compartments used for any particular purpose?" Yedidya asked without taking his eyes off a white butterfly that landed on a patch of grass and then fluttered away. "Why would anyone need to go up there?"

The question remained unanswered. The call of a coyote coming from the south made everyone freeze in place. Within a moment, though, they recovered their wits. The children had

---

7. Mishnah *Tamid* 3:7.

8. Mishnah *Middos* 4:7.

9. Ibid., 4:5.

The Kohanim's Entrance into the Heichal

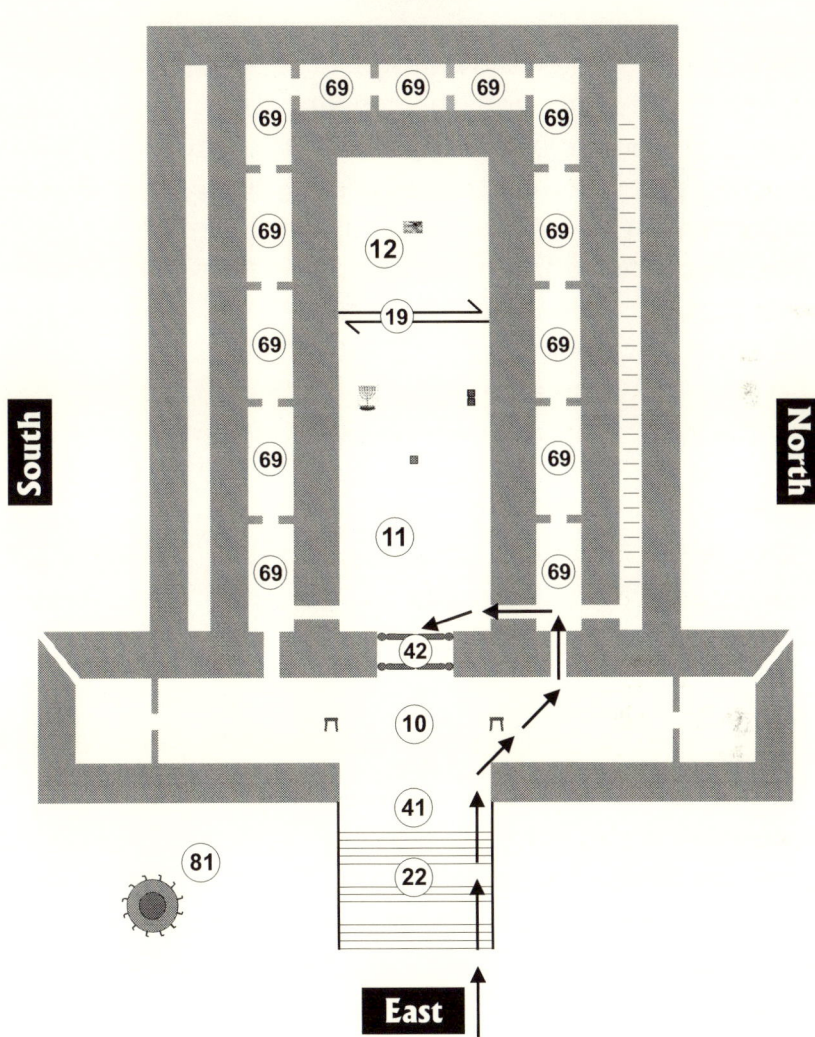

10. *Ulam*
11. *Heichal*
12. *Kodesh HaKodashim*
19. *Amah Teraksin* (two curtains and the passage between them that divided the *Heichal* from the *Kodesh HaKodashim*)

22. 12 Steps ascending to *Ulam*
41. Entrance to *Ulam*
42. Entrance to *Heichal*
69. Compartments
81. *Kiyor* (Washing Basin)

practiced often and they knew exactly what to do in a situation like this. In absolute silence, they rose from their places and quickly left the site.

Within two and a half minutes, everyone was safely huddled in the cave, except for the two lookouts, who would remain at their posts in the trees until the danger passed.

Up in his perch, concealed by the tree's thick leaves, Yossi watched a pair of Greeks approaching. They were dressed in hunting clothes, and when they got close enough he could see that they were carrying small animals that they had hunted. They passed through the clearing in the forest. Yossi saw one of them bend down and pick something up off the ground. The trees blocked his view and he couldn't see what it was. Because of the distance, he also couldn't hear their conversation.

*   *   *

"Look what a beautiful carving!" One Greek hunter held the precious model of the Beis HaMikdash in his hands and admired it. "It's truly a work of art! How in the world did it end up here?"

His friend took it and examined it from every angle. "Let's try to sell it in the market. Maybe we can get a few coins for it."

He then stuffed the miniature into his sack and the two men continued on their way to Yerushalayim.

*   *   *

Yossi and Boaz, the guards, slid quietly down from their posts and came back to the cave. Their *rebbi* and friends were already deeply engrossed in the lesson, as if they hadn't been suddenly interrupted.

Elkanah did a quick review for the sake of Yossi and Boaz and then said, "We learned that the *Mesibah* leads to the roof of the compartments, and Yedidya asked…yes, Yedidya, can you repeat your question?"

"Why do we need to go up to the roof of the compartments? What's there?" Yedidya reiterated.

Up in his perch, concealed by the tree's thick leaves,
Yossi watched a pair of Greeks approaching.

"On top of the *Heichal*(11) and the *Kodesh HaKodashim*(12) there is an attic(70), which is really another floor of the Beis HaMikdash. Someone who wants to go up to the attic climbs up the *Mesibah*(23) from east to west. When he gets to the northwestern corner of the *Heichal*, he turns left and continues walking above the western compartments until he reaches the next corner. He then turns left again and climbs up another *Mesibah* until he gets to the entrance of the attic, which is located on top of the southeastern corner of the *Heichal*."[10]

"How big is the attic?" wondered Shimon, shaking off the sand that stuck to his fingers.

"The attic is exactly the same size as the *Heichal* and the *Kodesh HaKodashim* that are under it.[11] It also has two *parochos* that separate between the space above the *Heichal* and the space above the *Kodesh HaKodashim*.[12]

"And what about the south of the *Heichal*? Is there a *Mesibah* there too?" Zevulun asked, curling his *peyos*, which had become unruly in the race back to the cave.

"No. There are three parallel walls on that side too, but the space between the outer wall and the second wall is used to drain the rainwater that accumulates on the roof of the attic, and it's called *Beis Horadas HaMayim*, the Drainage Channel(24).[13]

"We're finished for today, boys." Elkanah stood up and stretched his stiff limbs. "You have free time now."

The children scattered happily throughout the cave. It was only when Reuven and Yehudah sat down to plan the next stage of their model that they realized it was missing.

---

10. Ibid.
11. Ibid., 4:6.
12. *Kesubos* 106a.
13. Mishnah *Middos* 4:7.

The Staircase

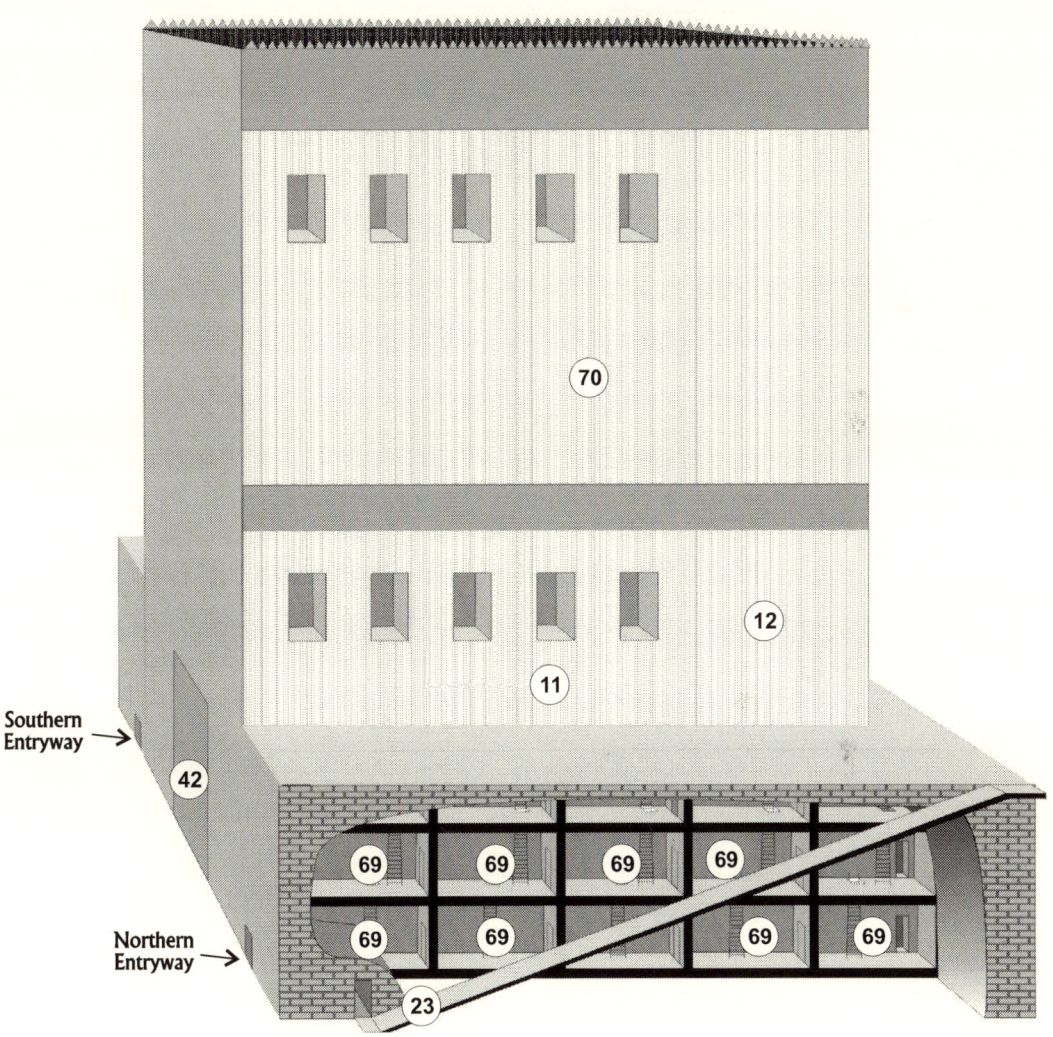

Southern
Entryway →

Northern
Entryway →

11. *Heichal*
12. *Kodesh HaKodashim*
23. Staircase

42. Entrance to *Heichal*
69. Compartments
70. Attic

The Compartments, Staircase, and Drainage Channel

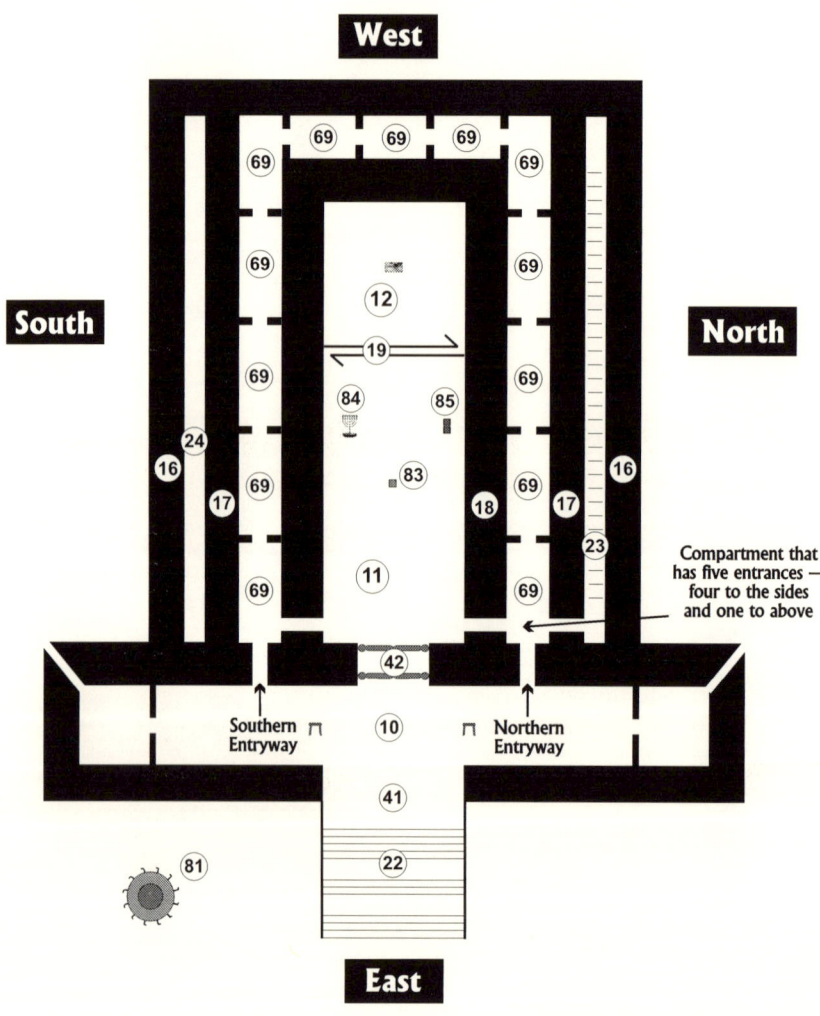

West

South

North

Compartment that
has five entrances —
four to the sides
and one to above

Southern
Entryway

Northern
Entryway

East

10. *Ulam*
11. *Heichal*
12. *Kodesh HaKodashim*
16. Wall of *Ulam*, Staircase, and
    Drainage Channel
17. Wall of Compartments (*Ta'im*)
18. Wall of *Heichal*
19. *Amah Teraksin* (two curtains and the
    passage between them that divided the
    Heichal from the *Kodesh HaKodashim*)

22. 12 Steps ascending to *Ulam*
23. Staircase
24. Drainage Channel
41. Entrance to *Ulam*
42. Entrance to *Heichal*
69. Compartments
81. *Kiyor* (Washing Basin)
83. The Golden (Incense) Altar
84. Menorah
85. Showbread Table

"Didn't you bring it back to the cave with you?" Reuven asked Yehudah nervously.

"I was sure that you were taking it," answered Yehudah ruefully.

"Has anyone seen the model? Does anyone know where it is?" Reuven called out in a strained voice.

No answer.

Worried, the boys went to Elkanah. "R…Rebbi, w…we can't find our model," stammered Yehudah.

"We want to go out and look for it," Reuven added, practically in tears. The replica was the most precious thing he had at the moment.

Yossi ran over to them. "When you went back to the cave, after I saw two Greeks coming and gave the signal, I watched the Greeks from up in the tree. I saw them pick something up from the ground in the clearing, but I couldn't see exactly what it was. I was too far away," he apologized.

Elkanah could see how important this was to the boys. "Come," he said. "I'll go with you."

But even the most thorough search along the path from the forest to the cave turned up nothing. The precious miniature was nowhere to be found.

Chapter Five

Feast of the Faithful

Crestfallen, the three returned to the cave. Reuven and Yehudah were feeling gloomy, pained by the loss of the replica of the Beis HaMikdash that they had worked on for months.

Elkanah was feeling down as well, but for a completely different reason.

"Boys!" he cried. The children quickly gathered around him. "I really hope that the missing miniature doesn't fall into the wrong hands. From now on, we'll have to be extra careful."

The children nodded in understanding.

"Reuven!" Yehudah stood up with a spark of determination in his eye. "Let's not give in to despair! We can't let ourselves be sad. Tomorrow we'll start building a new model, and 'the glory of this last House will be greater than the first.'[1] This time we'll make more room for the compartments on the sides of the *Heichal*."

Reuven lifted his head, and for the first time since the precious model was lost, a smile broke out on his face.

*   *   *

The awful news traveled fast along the Jewish street.

---

1. *Chaggai* 2:9.

46

"Did you hear? Another 'original' decree courtesy of the Greeks," reported one man with a bitter laugh. "Beginning today, anyone who owns a bull must write on its horn, 'We have no part in the God of Yisrael.'[2] Those wicked Greeks!" He shook his fist in the air and bit his lip, trying to control his temper. "But why are they interested specifically in the horn of a bull?"[3]

"In order to publicize it, and also to remind us of the *Cheit Ha-Eigel*,"[4] another man replied in a low voice.

"Do you understand the meaning of this cruel new decree? It means that anyone who fears Hashem will not be able to own cattle. After all, we won't write such heretical words on our animals. So where will we get milk from? And how will we plow our fields?"

This terrible question hung unanswered in the air.

Throughout the country, people began to hold large, lavish meals, consisting mainly of beef. Without a second thought, faithful Jews slaughtered their cows, one of their sole possessions that had escaped Greek plundering. The meat of these animals was served at big meals where families gathered to strengthen their belief in Hashem.

"You may ask what we are going to eat tomorrow," Elazar said, wiping his mouth and looking lovingly at the members of his family who were eating in silence. In their minds, they thought about days past, when they rejoiced as they ate the meat

---

2. Talmud Yerushalmi, *Chagigah* 2:2.

3. In those days they would make baby bottles out of animal horns; perhaps this decree expressed the Greeks' intention to inculcate Jewish children with heretical ideas from the time they were very young (Rav Leib Gurwicz *zt"l*, Gateshead Rosh Yeshiva, in *Aleinu L'Shabei'ach, Bereishis*, p. 81 [Hebrew]).

4. See commentaries to *Bereishis Rabbah* 2.

of *korbanos*.[5] Now, they had no pleasure from eating this meat. They were worried about the future, and Elazar had put their feelings into words. "We just slaughtered our cow, and now we cannot plow our field and grow grain. And if you ask, where will we get milk if we just consumed the cow that provided us with milk?"

The family members put down their forks and knives and looked wordlessly at their father, whose face was glowing with the joy of a mitzvah.

"I'll answer you with a parable.[6] This can be compared to a wealthy king who ruled over many countries. He owned vast properties and endless gold and silver. He lived an extravagant lifestyle, as befitting a king of his stature. One day, the king's servants caught a rare songbird that chirped the loveliest melodies. The same day that they caught the bird, the news reached the palace that a rebellion against the king was taking place on one of the kingdom's far-off islands.

"When the precious bird was taken to the king's courtyard in a golden cage, one of the lowest-ranking servants piped up and said, 'Have pity on the poor songbird! Who knows if we'll be able to give her any food to eat during and after the rebellion?'

"His friends laughed when they heard that. 'You fool!' they told him. 'Our great king rules over dozens of countries. His wealth is estimated in the millions of gold dinars, and you think that a rebellion of a few people at the end of the earth will make him into a pauper who can't even provide a few grains of wheat for a bird?!'

"That's the parable, and I'm sure you understood its message," Elazar's voice turned passionate and his face reddened

---

5. *Pesachim* 109a.

6. *Shemiras HaLashon, Sha'ar HeTevunah* 10.

with emotion. "The king is Hashem, the King of all kings, who rules over the heavens and earth and the entire universe. He keeps every being alive, from the tiniest creatures to the lofty angels who are so tall that it would take over five hundred years to walk their length.[7] He feeds and sustains them all, and you're worried that because of a few rebels in our little world, which is just a tiny speck in the enormous galaxy, we will lack sustenance? We, of all people, are close to the King and He wants only the best for us!"

A warm glow spread through the hearts of the family members seated around the table.

"'Trust in Hashem forever, because in Hashem is the strength of the worlds,'"[8] the oldest son raised his voice in song and everyone else joined in, strengthening their faith in Hashem and forgetting all about the dangers lurking outside. "Trust in Hashem forever, believe in Him always! He is the One who created two worlds with the two letters of His name. *Olam HaZeh*, this world, was created with the letter *heh* and *Olam HaBa*, the next world, was created with the letter *yud*.[9] HaKadosh Baruch Hu created two incredible worlds with just two letters! Is it not then a simple matter for Him to sustain all His creations?!"

*　　　*　　　*

The three Greek soldiers who burst into the house, swords drawn, brought their song to an instant stop.

"Where's the baby?" yelled the biggest of the three, who was nearly six feet six inches tall.

The terrified children cowered in their seats, and only Elazar answered. "What baby?" he asked in confusion.

---

7. *Chagigah* 13b.

8. *Yeshayahu* 26:4.

9. *Menachos* 29b.

"Well, what is this meal if not a circumcision celebration?" thundered the Greek. "And if there is a circumcision, there has to be a baby!" He laughed uproariously at his own little joke. One of the Greek decrees was that it was forbidden to perform a *bris milah* on a baby.[10]

"We didn't circumcise any baby here," said Elazar in a quiet but definitive voice.

"Liar! Men, search the entire house!" The soldiers fanned out, smashing and destroying everything in their path, tossing objects to the floor and helping themselves to anything that struck their fancy.

The riot lasted about ten minutes but felt like an eternity. Finally, the three men returned to the front room, where the family members sat rooted to their seats in fear.

"All right, Jew. I must admit that we didn't find a baby anywhere. But if so," he raised his voice threateningly, "what is the meaning of this festive meal you are enjoying on an ordinary weekday?!"

"We slaughtered our large cow, so we're holding this party. It's a great holiday for us," explained Elazar, his face shining.

The Greek scratched his head. He'd never heard of this particular Jewish festival, but the juicy steak that he was offered made him forget his puzzlement. The three soldiers enjoyed a few delicious pieces of meat, washed it down with some fine wine, and left the house at last.

"Trust in Hashem forever," the song went on, this time even more fervently than before.

*   *   *

The deputy chief of police left the main headquarters feeling despondent. Since orders were given two weeks ago to fill the

---

10. *Megillas Antiochus.* See also Rashi, *Sanhedrin* 32b, s.v. *sh'vua ha-ben.*

schools with the children of Perushim, they had found a total of fifteen hidden children who were dragged against their will to the Greek school. The lazy police officers hadn't put too much effort into fulfilling their mission, whereas the God-fearing Jews fought with their lives to protect the spiritual future of the children. The Greek's mission was a guaranteed failure.

This morning, Pelagios, the police chief, received a letter from the Ministry of Education which demanded to know why there were still children in hiding. The letter ended with a veiled threat that the police chief might soon find himself out of a job. Troubled, the police chief took his frustrations out on his deputy, blaming him for the fiasco.

Now the deputy plodded slowly through the streets, his mood bleak. In his despair, he didn't notice the residents who passed by and saluted him reverently. He had pinned all his hopes on the success of this mission, and he was sure that it would result in a major promotion. Perhaps he would be appointed chief of police in a different city in Eretz Yisrael! But now that he was being blamed for the mission's failure, all that seemed unlikely, to say the least.

Infuriated, he headed for the marketplace, looking for something he could buy for lunch, something that would lift his spirits a bit.

A makeshift stand on the corner caught his eyes. There was a table piled high with freshly killed rabbits, and Lapus the hunter sat behind it. The deputy fingered the animals, checking them for quality, and finally settled on one. He took a coin out of his money pouch and waited for change. The hunter searched inside his backpack after taking out the beautiful wood sculpture he had found in the forest and momentarily placing it on the table.

The officer saw the miniature and his eyes lit up. He knew how fond the police chief was of wooden miniatures.

"Tell me, please, how much are you selling that for?" he inquired, motioning toward the model.

After some brief negotiations, the two men settled on a price. The deputy left the stand, carrying lunch in his hand and hope in his heart that his gift would mollify his angry boss.

*   *   *

At the home of Matisyahu ben Yochanan the Kohen Gadol, a brave and fateful decision was reached: they would revolt and declare war against the Greeks. They would not allow Hashem's honor to be profaned!

Many long hours of deliberations preceded this decision, but finally, after consulting with other *gedolei Torah*, it was decided that in a time of *shmad* like this they were required to risk their lives to rid Eretz Yisrael of evil.

Matisyahu and his five sons, who were all great tzaddikim, would establish an army in which only G-d-fearing *talmidei chachamim* would serve. The *zechus* of their Torah and righteousness would help them succeed in battle.

The sons went from village to village, gathering soldiers for the army of Hashem.

"*Mi laShem eilay*! Whoever is for Hashem, join me!"[11] they rallied wherever they went.[12] They became known as Maccabim,[13] an acronym for their battle cry: "*Mi chamocha ba'eilim Hashem*! Who is like You, Hashem, among the powerful?"[14] But to their disappointment, only a few dozen Jews joined their cause.

"We're scared," many people apologized.

"According to halachah, we're not allowed to rebel against the Greeks," others defended their refusal to fight.

---

11. *Shemos* 32:26.
12. *Yosiphon* 20.
13. *Al HaTeshuos*, p. 117.
14. *Shemos* 15:11.

"Who is like You, Hashem, among the powerful?"

There were also those who simply shrugged their shoulders apathetically. The terrible *chillul HaShem* that was taking place did not sufficiently pain them and they saw no need to endanger their lives because of it.

There were also those who mocked their efforts. "Do you actually think you can create an army of *bnei Torah*? Torah learning saps a person's strength![15] Where will they find the strength to fight? And you think you're going to win…"

It was a good question, without a doubt. But the answer was even better, and it was not long in coming.

"Have you ever heard of Shimshon HaGibbor?"

"Who hasn't heard of him?" the doubters happily showed off their knowledge. "He killed a thousand Pelishtim in one day.[16] He also lifted off the gates of the city of Azza and carried them on his shoulders.[17] Okay, so what? He was a great *gibbor*, a mighty man. Not the sort you come across every day."

"Did you know that Shimshon was the judge and leader of Bnei Yisrael for twenty years?"[18] Matisyahu's sons rebuked them with fire in their eyes. "Everyone knows that in order to judge Bnei Yisrael you must be an expert in all areas of the Torah, learning and reviewing over and over; and you yourselves said that Torah drains a person's strength. Moreover, Shimshon was lame in both legs.[19] Clearly, his physical strength came from Hashem. How else could he defeat the Pelishtim? Strength and victory are from Hashem, and if He wills it, we can win, no matter how few and how weak we are!"

---

15. *Sanhedrin* 26b.

16. *Shoftim* 15:16.

17. Ibid., 16:3.

18. Ibid., 16:31.

19. *Sotah* 10a.

Chapter Six

In Search of the Miniature

I n their quest to sever the Jews from their religion, the Greeks decreed that *kiddush ha-chodesh*, the sanctification of the new month, was forbidden.[1] In those days, there was no set Jewish calendar. *Beis Din* would declare a new month based on the testimony of two witnesses who saw the new moon.[2] After two witnesses came and their testimony was checked and verified, Rosh Chodesh was declared.

Even after the Greeks came to power, the Jews, of course, continued with *kiddush ha-chodesh*, as they had done for generations. They did not follow the Greek calendar, and the Greeks could not tolerate that. They knew that all the Jewish holidays were determined by the Jewish calendar, and if the Jews stopped sanctifying the new month and started calculating dates like the Greeks, they would find it difficult, if not impossible, to keep their holidays.

Predictably, the Sages of the Sanhedrin were not deterred by the new decree, despite the death penalty that came along with it. Obviously, they could not hold their proceedings out in the open in the *Lishkas HaGazis*(53) as they normally did, but from a

---

1. *Bnei Yissaschar, Chodesh Kislev* 13.
2. *Rosh Hashanah* 18a–26a.

55

secluded location they continued to sanctify the months. It was a complicated operation. *Beis Din's* hiding place had to remain a secret so that the Greeks would not discover it. At the same time, the location had to be known to the witnesses who wanted to testify about the new moon they had spotted.[3]

In addition, once Rosh Chodesh was declared, messengers of *Beis Din* hurried throughout the land to inform the people.[4] There were months when it was crucial for the people to know when Rosh Chodesh was. For example, in the month of Nissan, if people were not informed of the date, they might inadvertently eat *chametz* on Pesach. Similarly, if the people did not know when Rosh Chodesh Tishrei fell out, they might eat on Yom Kippur.

So *Beis Din* continued to operate underground, even though their job seemed nearly impossible. Witnesses still came, messengers still spread the news of Rosh Chodesh, and the Greeks, despite their failures, still made every effort to uncover *Beis Din's* secret location.

The Greek police established a special task force to handle the mission to abolish *kiddush ha-chodesh*. This crew put undercover agents on the job, analyzed facts and fragments of rumors, and worked hard to achieve their goal. Yet every month, they were disappointed all over again.

*   *   *

What was the procedure for *kiddush ha-chodesh*?

If the moon was seen on the evening of the thirtieth of the month, and reliable witnesses testified to that effect, the month was sanctified on that day, which then became the first day of

---

3. Ibid., 23b.
4. Ibid., 18a.

the new month. The result was that the previous month had only twenty-nine days.[5] In this case, the calendar would go like this (for Nissan–Iyar): 28 Nissan, 29 Nissan, 1 Iyar, 2 Iyar…

If the new moon still had not been sighted on the evening of the thirtieth, the new month would not be sanctified on that day.[6] The previous month would end the next day, after thirty days, and the new month would begin on the thirty-first day.[7] In this case, the calendar would go like this: 28 Nissan, 29 Nissan, 30 Nissan, 1 Iyar, 2 Iyar…

The Greeks heard the news from one of their undercover detectives: foiled again! The Jewish Sages had managed to sanctify the month right under their noses!

Once, a messenger of *Beis Din* was caught. The police chief was sure that he had succeeded, when, after terrible torture, the messenger revealed *Beis Din*'s hiding place. His confidence was premature, however. At the end of the month, the chief himself showed up at the place, accompanied by a fully armed battalion of soldiers, only to find an empty house…

For safety reasons, the Sages changed their hiding place and the make-up of *dayanim* every month. The halachah which states that for *kiddush ha-chodesh* it is enough to have three *dayanim*[8] aided them in their fight against Greece, and with Hashem's help they were victorious again and again.

*   *   *

A clunky pair of feet, clad in shiny boots, was propped on an elegant wooden footrest. Pelagios, the Greek chief of police, sat in

---

5. Rambam, *Hilchos Kiddush HaChodesh* 1:6.

6. *Rosh Hashanah* 24a.

7. Rambam, *Hilchos Kiddush HaChodesh* 1:3.

8. *Sanhedrin* 2a.

his comfortable armchair and sank into the soft upholstery. The house, which he had appropriated for himself, used to belong to one of the richest men in Yerushalayim. One visit to the home was enough to convince Pelagios that this house had to be his, no matter what. He falsely accused the owner, Reb Binyamin, of various crimes. Binyamin was sold into slavery, and the rest of the family was cruelly evicted from their home. One of these family members was Reb Binyamin's son Reuven, who was one of the boys living in the cave under Elkanah's supervision.

Now Pelagios relaxed in his stolen armchair, filling his lungs with the fresh air that blew in through the wide windows and admiring the delicate wooden sculpture in his hand. The gift he had received from his deputy was exactly his taste and made him briefly forget about the difficulties he faced in his chase after the Jews. He examined the miniature from every angle, and a tiny engraving on the bottom caught his eye. "Reuven and Yehudah from Yerushalayim," he read with great difficulty.

"Jews!" he grumbled in annoyance. "You're here, too?!"

"This structure is familiar to me," he said out loud to himself, searching his memory. "Three large rooms, with two curtains in the middle. Where did I see such a thing? Maybe this is a model of the home of the boys who signed their names on the bottom? I think I'll ask my assistant to find a building like this and I'll take ownership of it. The eight rooms in this house here are not bad for living in, but I need someplace else to hold parties and gatherings for my friends."

He didn't know that Reuven's house was the one he had already taken for himself, the one he was living in at the moment.

Through the open doorway, a hand holding a steaming tray appeared. The hand was followed by its owner, the chief's assistant, a *misyavein* named Augustus.

Augustus bowed slightly and laid the tray on the low table next to the armchair, and then noticed the miniature in his master's hand.

"Where did you get such a lovely model of the Beis HaMik-dash?" he asked, instinctively reaching out to touch it.

"This is what the Beis HaMikdash looks like?" Pelagios was both surprised and disappointed. The Greek ruler surely would never grant him ownership of a place that had been turned into a shrine for idol worship. Too bad; he would have to give up his plan of hosting parties there.

"Yes," replied Augustus, oblivious to the thoughts flitting through his master's head. "The first room, that long one there, is called the *Ulam*(10). Behind these doors is the *Heichal*(11), which houses three vessels that are holy to the Jews: the *Shulchan*(85), the Menorah(84), and the *Mizbeach*(83). This curtain here is called the *paroches*(19), and the *Kodesh HaKodashim* is behind it."[9]

"And what's there?" the chief leaned forward, curious.

His assistant chuckled. "The truth? I don't know myself. I've never been inside. I don't observe the mitzvos anymore, but a little bit of the Jewish education I received has stayed with me. I'm afraid to go into that place. If you'd like, I can take you to the Beis HaMikdash tomorrow and you can go inside yourself and see that it looks just like this. I assume that the vessels I mentioned are no longer there; they were probably plundered by the illustrious Greek army."

*   *   *

"Where did you find it?" was the chief's first question when he walked into headquarters the next morning.

"Find what?" The deputy looked at his boss in alarm. Who knew what he was going to blame him for this time?

"That miniature house you gave me as a gift!"

"Oh, that," the deputy breathed a sigh of relief. "I bought it from Lapus the hunter."

---

9. Mishnah *Middos* 4:7.

"What does a hunter have to do with artwork like that? Summon him immediately! I'd like to have a word with him."

A short time later, Lapus, trembling in fear, appeared before the venerated police chief.

"Who did you steal that model from, you crook?" the chief roared at him.

"I didn't steal it, sir. I found it on a rock in the middle of the forest one day when Butrus and I went out hunting."

"Yeah, right, save your stories for your grandmother! You…" he stopped midsentence. A radical thought had just popped into the chief's head and it wouldn't go away. Perhaps there was a group of Jewish children hiding in the area! Maybe they were learning Torah in secret and had accidentally lost the model they used for their studies! The more he thought about it, the more it made sense.

"I want to hear *exactly* where you found this carving." The chief's now-soft tone took Lapus by surprise. He didn't know if the chief had really calmed down or if it was some kind of trick designed to get information out of him. In any case, he had no reason to lie.

"Butrus and I wanted to rest for a minute, because we were carrying all the rabbits we had hunted and they were heavy. We went into a clearing in the forest, which we had found on one of our earlier outings. It's about a two-hour walk from Yerushalayim," explained Lapus. "I noticed a nice wooden miniature on one of the rocks and figured it didn't belong to anyone. I'm happy to put it back there if you want," he offered.

"There's no need," said the police chief. "I just want you to come with us tomorrow so you can show my officers exactly where this clearing is."

Lapus nodded agreeably and left, his relief evident.

The chief fingered the miniature in amazement. "Such talent!" he said with a low whistle. "Children with hands like this have a great future! They really must study in our art college. Wouldn't it be a shame to waste such talent?" he asked his deputy, who nodded his enthusiastic agreement.

"Listen! Tomorrow you're going out to that area, and you're to leave no stone unturned! Tomorrow night I want those children over here. Understood?!"

*   *   *

On the morning of the twenty-third of Cheshvan, the skies were grayer than usual. When the deputy and his men left headquarters, there was already a light drizzle falling, but by the time they reached the clearing in the forest the drizzle had turned to a downpour. The driving rainstorm erased all footprints and made it difficult for the hunters to find the place they were looking for.

Only after a long search in the pouring rain did they find the exact spot. They quickly located a cave in the area, as well. The officers drew their swords and entered the cave, ready for battle, only to discover, to their great consternation, that it was empty. Soaked to the bone, they sat down in the cave and decided to rest a little and warm up until the rain stopped.

"We can't continue like this!" said one strapping officer. His friends nodded their agreement. It only stopped raining three hours later.

"We're going back now," decided the deputy. "You'd all better promise not to tell the chief how many hours we spent searching and how many hours we rested in the cave."

*   *   *

From the window of his well-heated room, the chief watched the streams of water rushing through the streets, and he knew that his men would return empty-handed.

"It's all right," he said, to their surprise, when they showed up back at headquarters and stammered their apologies. "We'll wait for a nice, sunny day and then I'll go myself. Those little Jews won't escape my clutches."

Chapter Seven

A Special Lesson

28 MARCHESHVAN, 3622. OUTSIDE THE WALLS OF YERUSHALAYIM.

A lone pedestrian, leading two donkeys, headed briskly down the road that led to Yaffo. Yochanan was laden with food and supplies for the children in hiding. After half an hour of walking on the main road, he turned onto a dirt path concealed by trees. Two pairs of burning eyes, following his every move, lit up.

Yochanan continued uphill on the path, unaware that he was being followed. He walked that way for an hour and a half, wiping away the beads of sweat that appeared on his forehead. When they reached the cave, the donkeys came to a stop. The brush was too thick and they couldn't continue walking.

Yochanan tied the animals to a thick tree trunk by their reins, lifted three overflowing baskets in each hand, and squeezed through the dense forest growth. The detectives stayed about fifty yards away, hunched behind a low ridge, listening intently.

"Yochanan is here!" they could hear a child's excited cry.

"Did you bring me a letter from my parents?" came another jubilant voice, carried by the wind straight to the Greeks' ears.

"Boaz, they sent you some of those yummy cakes again!"

The detectives didn't need to hear any more. Mission accomplished.

*　　　*　　　*

At police headquarters, the chief listened carefully to the report and clasped his hands in satisfaction.

"Excellent, excellent! You did a wonderful job!" he complimented the two men who beamed with unconcealed pride. "Tomorrow I'll go there myself to catch those children! They won't slip through my fingers this time!"

29 MARCHESHVAN. 5:30 A.M.

Elkanah was wide awake and had already immersed in the small mikveh in the corner of the cave. The children arose, as always, before dawn. They washed their hands and got dressed, and then began to daven *Shacharis*. Elkanah had trained his students to daven at sunrise, *k'vasikin*. "It's worthwhile to do so not only because of the great value of praying at sunrise,"[1] he explained to them the day after they arrived at the cave, "but also because we don't have a *minyan*, and davening *k'vasikin* takes precedence over davening with a *minyan*."[2]

The children had no idea what lay ahead. They didn't know how long this day would be and how much upheaval they would experience before they could finally go to sleep…

Breakfast after davening was especially delicious, because the bread was fresh this time. "It was baked just yesterday!" Mahalalel announced what everyone already knew. What they didn't know was that this was the last breakfast they would eat in this cave, their home for the last six months.

*   *   *

"Today we're going to learn about *kiddush ha-chodesh*," Elkanah began. The boys sat up straighter and listened intently. "I decided

---

1. *Berachos* 9b, with *Tosfos* s.v. *kol ha-someich*.
2. *Bei'ur Halachah* 58:1, s.v. *u'mitzvah min hamuvchaar*.

to focus on this topic for two reasons. First of all, tomorrow, it seems, will be declared Rosh Chodesh, and *'davar b'ito mah tov,'*[3] it is always nice to learn about a subject in its proper time. I want you to understand how the system works. Second of all, the Greeks want to eradicate the mitzvah of *kiddush ha-chodesh,*[4] so we will focus our energies specifically on that mitzvah."

"How does Rebbi know that tomorrow is going to be Rosh Chodesh?" Yedidya wondered. He peered up at the slice of heaven that was visible from the opening of the cave. Who knew? Maybe he would spot the new moon?

"I'm not a hundred percent sure, but according to the calculation of the months, I assume it will be so. Tishrei was *malei,* a full month of thirty days, so Cheshvan will probably be *chaser,* a short month of twenty-nine days. Today is the twenty-ninth, and there's a good chance that towards evening the new moon will be visible."

"But why not make all the months the same number of days?" Naftali stopped scraping at the dried mud that stuck to his clothes and looked at his teacher. "Why are some months longer and some months shorter?"

"I'll try to explain as best as I can, but in order to understand you'll have to concentrate. Reuven!" Ekanah addressed his student. "You're rather distracted today. It seems to me that you're busy thinking about the new miniature you finished building yesterday. Am I correct?"

Reuven looked up in surprise. "How does the Rebbi know what I'm thinking about?"

Elkanah gave a mysterious smile and didn't answer. It was the sort of thing that only another teacher could understand. He didn't tell Reuven, but the boy's fingers climbing in the air, as if

---

3. *Mishlei* 15:23.

4. *Megillas Antiochus.*

going up a ladder from compartment to compartment, gave away the secret.

"So, boys, shall we begin? Is everyone ready?"

"Yes! Sounds so interesting…" came a babble of voices. Then quiet reigned once more and Elkanah began to speak.

"When Hashem first told Moshe the laws of *korban Pesach,* He said, 'This month shall be for you the first month.'[5] From the word 'this,' the Sages learned out, 'Like *this* you should see and sanctify.'[6] In other words, HaKadosh Baruch Hu showed Moshe the new moon and told him, 'When you see the moon looking exactly like this, sanctify it.' I'll explain to you what Moshe saw, and how the moon is sanctified.

"As we all know, at the beginning of the month the moon is small, even very small. It's really just a narrow sliver. As the month goes on, it grows larger and larger. On the seventh of the month, the moon is a semicircle. On the fourteenth and fifteenth of the month, there is a full moon, and from then on the moon begins to wane. It gets smaller and smaller, until on the twenty-second of the month we see only half of it; towards the end of the month it's just a small sliver again; and at the end it disappears completely."

"I have a question." Shimshon broke the silence. "Does the moon really get bigger and smaller? It actually disappears? How does that happen?"

"The moon itself is always the same size. What changes is the part of the moon that is illuminated."

"Really? I thought it was the moon itself, growing and shrinking miraculously!" Shimshon laughed, and his friends laughed along with him.

---

5. *Shemos* 12:2.
6. Rashi, ibid.

Their teacher gently shushed them. "When Hashem created the world, He created 'the two big luminaries,'[7] — the moon and the sun — equal in size. The moon came to Hashem and complained, 'Two kings cannot share one crown.' HaKadosh Baruch Hu then told the moon, 'Go and make yourself smaller!'[8] Hashem was telling the moon that until now it gave off light like the sun. Once the moon complained, however, it no longer had any light of its own and was only able to receive and reflect the light of the sun."[9]

Elkanah shifted his position on the rock. "Since the moon is only illuminated by light from the sun, the side of the moon that faces the sun is always lit up, while the other side is always dark.[10] Over the course of a month, the moon completes one orbit around Earth. During this orbit, we sometimes see part of the bright side of the moon. Other times we see the entire bright side; that's when there's a full moon."

A little lizard skittered past and disappeared into an invisible hole.

Now Elkanah reached the main point he wanted to clarify to his students. "In every month there are about two days when we don't see the moon at all, because it is between the sun and Earth and only the dark side of the moon faces us.[11] After a little while, the moon slowly moves away from the sun towards the east, and then we can see a small sliver of the moon. That is what Hashem showed Moshe Rabbeinu. One who sees the moon in that form can go to *Beis Din* and testify."

*   *   *

---

7. *Bereishis* 1:16.

8. *Chullin* 60b.

9. Rabbeinu Bachya, *Bereishis* 1:14.

10. *Peirush* to Rambam, *Hilchos Kiddush HaChodesh* 1:3.

11. Rambam, *Hilchos Kiddush HaChodesh* 1:3.

All throughout the morning, while the children were busy with their studies, feverish preparations were taking place in Yerushalayim. The chief of police was mobilizing his men for a surprise attack on the cave. Thirty strapping officers were chosen for the task and outfitted with everything they needed.

"You will not let a single child escape!" he warned them constantly.

After repeating the same things so many times and spending so much time talking, the chief was feeling hungry. The aromas that wafted from the headquarters' kitchen only reinforced what his stomach was already telling him: it was time for lunch. Pelagios was not one to miss such an important daily event! He sat down to eat, making sure to sample every single dish that was offered and drink every cup of wine. Predictably, the hearty meal made him rather drowsy and he sat down in an armchair for a little nap.

After an hour of deep sleep, he woke up refreshed and energetic. As nimbly as he could, considering his hefty proportions, he left the house and joined the officers waiting outside. Their grumbling about how long they had been waiting for him went right over his head.

"Let's go, men! Time for the big raid!" he declared, and the group was on its way.

*   *   *

Only a few congregants remained in the little *beis ha-knesses*. Yehudah ben Matisyahu sat down on a hard wooden bench, exhaustion filling his every limb. It was over a week now that he had been traveling from town to town and from village to village to gather an army of God-fearing men and awaken those Jews who had fallen into a state of apathy.

An older man approached him and shook his hand warmly. "Name's Menashe," he introduced himself. "From the descendants of Machir ben Menashe. I want to know where our fighters are supposed to assemble. I may not be a young man anymore, but I want to use every ounce of strength I have left for *kevod Shamayim*!"

Yehudah clasped his hand firmly. "*Yasher koach*, Jew! Go to Mount Moda'is.[12] You'll find my father there, and he'll tell you what to do next."

"Within two weeks, we're going to revolt," mused Yehudah while riding to the next village. A colorful songbird fluttered next to his hand, chirping happily in his ear.

But the revolt began earlier than expected.

*   *   *

The Greek ruler Philippos heard that a Jewish rebellion was brewing. "Good" Jews had taken the trouble to report the news to him. These were *misyavnim*, Hellenistic Jews, former Tzedokim, who the Perushim referred to as "*paritzim*." These *misyavnim* drew much pleasure and satisfaction from the Greek rule, and they cast off the mitzvos, which they viewed as burdensome. Instead of learning Torah and keeping Shabbos, they played sports and watched plays and bullfights. The Jewish *batei din* had been shut down, and they could do as they pleased.

The *misyavnim* were pleased with the way things were now, and when they heard about the upcoming rebellion, they were eager to do everything in their power to nip it in the bud. They even told Philippos that old Matisyahu ben Yochanan Kohen Gadol was the leader of the movement, and his sons were traveling around the country to recruit supporters for their cause.

Philippos seethed with fury, though he wasn't particularly worried. A bunch of feeble old men and scrawny kids; what could they do already? He knew that this silly rebellion would be suppressed as soon as it started.

---

12. *Yosiphon* 20.

Chapter Eight

Narrow Escape

29 MARCHESHVAN. 3:00 P.M.

The children washed their faces with cool spring water and sat down in the "classroom" refreshed and ready to continue learning after their afternoon break.

"Now we finally come to the secret of *kiddush ha-chodesh*," whispered Elkanah in a mysterious voice. "The time when the new moon appears is called that month's *molad*. The span of time between the *molad* of one month and the *molad* of the next month is not fixed.[1] Only the Sages of the Sanhedrin, with their great knowledge, know how to calculate when the *molad* of the next month will be.[2] Therefore, if at the end of the twenty-ninth day of the month, after sunset, two Jews see a small sliver of the new moon, they hurry to *Beis Din*, where they are thoroughly questioned.[3] If their testimony matches the Sanhedrin's calculations, because enough time has passed since the last *molad* for the new moon to be visible the way the witnesses said it was, then their testimony is accepted and *Beis Din* sanctifies the new month."

---

1. Rambam, *Hilchos Kiddush HaChodesh* 17:23.
2. Ibid., chapters 11–19.
3. *Rosh Hashanah* 23b.

"What would we do if *chas v'shalom* the Greeks do manage to abolish *kiddush ha-chodesh*?" Mahalalel was very worried. "How will we have all of the *Yamim Tovim*?"

"It would be very sad," said Elkanah, his face turning serious. "But even if that does happen, all is not lost. We have a tradition passed down to us, *halachah l'Moshe mi'Sinai*, that there are two ways to sanctify the month.[4] One is the way that we use now: two witnesses testify that they saw the new moon and *Beis Din* sanctifies the month. But there's another way."

Yehudah stood up in place so he could concentrate better.

"The second way is that *Beis Din* can calculate the *average* time span between one *molad* and the next, and based on that they can establish a fixed calendar even for the next thousand years."[5]

"What is that average time span?" Yehudah couldn't resist asking.

"Twenty-nine days, twelve hours and seven hundred and ninety-three *chalakim*."[6]

"What do you mean, '*chalakim*'? Why not minutes?" Zevulun, who was sitting quietly until now, suddenly piped up.

"The calculation of the *molad* is extremely precise. For the purposes of these calculations, every hour is divided into one thousand and eight *chalakim*.[7] In other words, one minute contains eighteen *chalakim*. $1080 \div 60 = 18$."

"Now I finally understand why some months are *malei*, with thirty days, and other months are *chaser*, with twenty-nine months," Shimshon clapped his hands in joy. "It's because the average length of a month is twenty-nine and a half days!"

---

4. Rambam, *Hilchos Kiddush HaChodesh* 5:1–3.

5. This is the method for setting the Jewish calendar that we use today.

6. Rambam, *Hilchos Kiddush HaChodesh* 6:3.

7. Ibid., 6:2.

"Not quite," Zechariah corrected him. "You forgot that there are an extra seven hundred and...seven hundred and..."

"And ninety-three *chalakim*," Naftali came to his rescue.

"Which equal about three-quarters of an hour. That's why there are more months that are *malei* than *chaser*," finished off the *rebbi*. He stood up, his head nearly reaching the roof of the cave, and announced dramatically, "Today is Tuesday, the twenty-ninth day of Marcheshvan. In about two hours, the sun will set. If Jews see the new moon, *Beis Din* will sanctify the new month based on their testimony, and tomorrow, Wednesday, will be the first of Kislev. But if witnesses don't see the new moon tonight, tomorrow will be the thirtieth of Cheshvan, and Rosh Chodesh Kislev will be on Thursday. When Yochanan comes here before Shabbos, he'll let us know what *Beis Din* decided."

The children nodded, pleased that the concepts they'd grown up with but never really understood now made perfect sense. None of them had any idea that this time Yochanan would not be the one to inform them of the date of Rosh Chodesh...

"The Greeks are very upset about the existence of the Jewish calendar," added the *rebbi*, sitting down carefully. "They want us to calculate the date based on the sun, the way they do.[8] But we will continue to establish our calendar based on the moon, the way we've always done.

"Do you know, children? Our existence here on earth is similar to the moon. Now we are in a state of darkness and lowliness, and from here on we hope to rise up again and return to our former brightness."

"My father once told me a beautiful idea," Reuven said, his voice breaking at the mention of his father. "From Avraham Avinu until Shlomo HaMelech there were fifteen generations.

---

8. *Sukkah* 29a.

During that time, the light of the Jewish people shone brighter and brighter, reaching its climax during the reign of Shlomo, the wisest of all men and builder of the Beis HaMikdash. These fifteen generations correspond to the first fifteen days of the month. From that point on, things regressed, and our light grew dimmer during the reign of the fifteen kings from Shlomo until the last king, Tzidkiyahu, whose eyes were blinded by Nevuchadnetzar.[9] It was during Tzidkiyahu's time that the First Beis HaMikdash was destroyed."[10]

Impressed, Elkanah clasped Reuven on the shoulder in admiration.

3:40 P.M.

About an hour's march from the cave, a cloud of dust gathered in the air. Riding on a horse, accompanied by his officers on foot, Pelagios headed to the cave, his detectives leading the way.

3:45 P.M.

"Is it true that the Kusim would interfere with *kiddush ha-chodesh*?" asked Yedidya.

"They did cause trouble, but not because they made it difficult for *Beis Din* to sanctify the month. Instead, they tried to disrupt the method used to spread the news of Rosh Chodesh. Once *Beis Din* declares a new month, they have to let everyone know, including the Jews in faraway Bavel.[11] In the past, they would use a very efficient system by which the news would reach Bavel within minutes." Elkanah paused and gave a worried glance at Yossi. "It looks like you're not feeling well, Yossi. Is everything okay?"

---

9. *II Melachim* 25:7.
10. *Shemos Rabbah* 15:26.
11. *Rosh Hashanah* 18a.

"My head hurts," answered Yossi quietly, resting his head on the wall of the cave. "It's all right, the Rebbi should continue, please."

Elkanah looked at him nervously, but went on. "Four tall mountains between Eretz Yisrael and Bavel were chosen for this purpose. A messenger of *Beis Din* would stand on Har HaZeisim, also called Har HaMishchah, where he had long beams of cedar woods wrapped in reeds, balsam wood, and flax combings. He would light this enormous torch and wave it back and forth and up and down, over and over again.

"Another messenger, who was already waiting on the second mountain, which was Mount Sartava on the other side of the Yarden River, would see the signal and light a similar torch. He would wave his torch to signal the messenger on the third mountain, Mount Grufina, to light his torch. The third messenger would then signal to the fourth messenger who was waiting on Mount Chavran. From there, the news spread in a similar fashion to Beis Baltin. There, opposite the Jewish community in Bavel, the messenger waved his enormous torch and when the Babylonian Jews saw the signal they would also climb up to the roofs of their houses and lift up torches until the entire Diaspora was lit up like a big bonfire. That's how the messenger knew that his message had been received."[12]

"What night would they light the torches?" asked Mahalalel.

"An excellent question," the *rebbi* complimented him. "*Beis Din* does not sanctify the month at night, so after witnesses came on the evening of the thirtieth, the members of *Beis Din* waited until the next day and declared Rosh Chodesh. They then sent out the message at night, which was already the night of the second of the month. The Jews in the Diaspora knew that the mountaintop

---

12. *Rosh Hashanah* 22b.

signal meant that it was already the second of the month, and the previous day had been Rosh Chodesh. After a *chodesh malei* of thirty days, they would not light torches, and the Jews of Bavel knew that the day after the thirtieth had to be the first of the new month."

"So what did those Kusim do?" Yedidya, who had been waiting patiently until now, repeated his question.

The *rebbi* waved his finger in Yedidya's direction. "Thank you for reminding me. The Kusim wanted to confuse the people in the Diaspora, so they came up with a very simple plan. On one of the full, thirty-day months, when torches are not lit, the Kusim went up to the top of one of their mountains north of Yerushalayim, and lit torches. The messenger of *Beis Din* who was waiting on Mount Sartava saw the signal and didn't realize that it was a trick. He lit his torch, and from there the mistaken message reached Bavel, and as a result of that the Jews there thought Rosh Chodesh was a day earlier than it actually was. After this incident, the news of *kiddush ha-chodesh* was always delivered in person by messengers of *Beis Din*."[13]

The *rebbi* laughed lightly. "Just from the number of enemies who try to undermine it, we can see the tremendous importance of this mitzvah. First there were the Kusim, then the Baitosim, and now the Greeks..."

The children's curiosity was piqued. What did the Baitosim do?

Elkanah stretched out his legs. "Once, the Baitosim wanted to trick the Sages, so they hired two men whom they paid two hundred *zuzim* each. They instructed them to go to *Beis Din* and falsely testify that they had seen the new moon. The Baitosim spent a lot of time teaching these two false witnesses the answers

---

13. Rashi, ibid., s.v. *mi'shekilkelu*.

to the questions that *Beis Din* would ask, so that no one would suspect them of being fakes.

"The evening of the thirtieth arrived, and the two men arrived at *Beis Din* full of confidence. The first witness was interrogated by *Beis Din*. He answered all the questions perfectly, and the *Beis Din* was convinced that he was telling the truth.

"When the second witness came in, he said, 'I was approaching Ma'aleh Adumim, and I saw the moon crouching between two rocks. Its head looked like the head of a calf, its ears like the ears of a goat, its horns were like the horns of a deer, and its tail rested between its legs.'

"The Sages listened to this strange description, trying to understand what this man was telling them.

"'I looked at the moon and I was startled, so I jumped back,' the man finished his testimony. He waited a few minutes and then continued. 'Just so that you'll believe what I'm saying, I'll show you the sack of money that I received from the Baitosim in exchange for my false testimony.'

"'And why did you come to testify?' the Sages asked him.

"'I heard that they were looking for false witnesses and I decided to offer my services in order to foil their plot and expose their deception.'

"The Sages told him, 'Keep the two hundred *zuzim* as a gift for you, and the man who hired you will be punished with lashes.'

"From that day on, *Beis Din* would only accept witnesses who they knew to be trustworthy."[14]

4:10 P.M.

The dust cloud came closer and closer to the cave, but its young inhabitants were completely unaware of the approaching danger.

---

14. *Rosh Hashanah* 22b.

Pelagios and his officers were half an hour away.

"I will take the children who built that model and supervise them myself," decided Pelagios. "I, with my very own hands, will put them in our excellent Greek school. They'll study art, and with talent like theirs I'm sure they'll go far!"

4:20 P.M.

When *Minchah* was over, there was a special surprise waiting for the boys. "Since the skies have cleared up and the clouds are gone, we'll go up to the top of the mountain now," Elkanah told the children, who responded with squeals of delight. "According to my calculations, the moon may appear in less than half an hour. Put on your coats and let's go. It'll take us twenty-five minutes to reach the top of the mountain."

"We'll be walking back in the dark?" asked Mahalalel. "I'm afraid I'm going to trip."

"I hope that we'll see the moon shortly after sunset, and we'll make it back before dark," Elkanah reassured him. There was something else that worried him, though. "Yossi, do you want to come or stay behind?"

Yossi blushed as all the boys looked at him. "I would love to come, but I think I'd better stay here and rest. My head hurts terribly. I could hardly listen to today's lesson."

"I'll stay with you," Reuven offered generously. "I'm sure I'll have plenty of other opportunities to see the moon."

4:25 P.M.

Ten small figures and one large figure could be seen climbing up the mountain. The afternoon sun illuminated their faces with an orange glow and colored their hair golden.

Inside the cave, Yossi lay down on his bed of straw with a sigh of relief, closing his eyes in exhaustion. Reuven sat down next to the table, picked up his delicate knife and began to carve out another miniature ladder. Taking advantage of the utter quiet in the cave, he became totally engrossed in his work.

4:39 P.M.

The sound of crunching leaves came from the entrance of the cave. Reuven looked up in surprise.

"They're back already?" Yossi asked drowsily.

"They can't be," said Reuven, worried. "According to my estimate, they left about fifteen minutes ago. Not more. It'll take at least that long for them to reach the top of the mountain."

"Shh..." Yossi sat up in bed, tense. "Listen!"

Reuven cocked his head in concentration and then turned pale. "They're talking in Greek!"

They grabbed each other, trembling in fear. Yossi's headache was completely forgotten. They were alone, against...who knew? They didn't know who these approaching strangers were, but they could guess why they were coming.

"Where can we hide?"

"Come, fast, we'll go behind those mattresses!"

"They'll find us in a minute," whispered Yossi through chattering teeth. The voices were getting closer and Reuven had to think fast.

"Quick, quick, what do we do? Oh! I know!" He grabbed Yossi hard by the arm and pulled him over to the chimney shaft.

"We'll escape through here! Go in, fast!" Yossi pushed himself in while Reuven helped him from behind, and he began to crawl on his stomach. The shaft was narrow, just wide enough for a child, and it was about fifty feet long. Reuven climbed in, too, just as two officers appeared at the entrance to the cave holding flaming torches.

"Faster, faster," Reuven told himself. His knees knocked together, and it took all the strength he could muster to get into the tunnel.

Yossi pushed himself in while Reuven helped him from behind.

Pelagios entered the cave. His eyes immediately lit on the new model of the Beis HaMikdash on the table, and he knew that this time he was on target. They had come to the right place.

"Where are the children?" he bellowed at the officers. "Look for them! Catch them immediately!"

A slight movement from the direction of the shaft caught the attention of one of the officers.

"What's that over there? It's a boy's foot!"

"Catch him now!" roared the chief of police.

The officer leapt over to the shaft but he was a second too late. The foot disappeared into the shaft. Inside were two boys, crawling with all their might, their bodies drenched in sweat.

"Why are you standing there like an idiot? Follow him! Get him!" Pelagios was nearly hysterical.

The officer tried to shove his way inside, but three feet in he got stuck. The passageway was too small for a man his size.

His friends pulled him out and pushed in the skinniest officer instead, but he couldn't get too far, either. After six or seven feet, he gave up and came back out.

"It's impossible; the shaft is too narrow."

The chief of police went wild. "What is this supposed to be? What is all this bumbling around? Heads will roll because of this! How did they know we were coming? Who leaked the information?!"

He stomped his feet, grabbed every object in sight and threw it on the floor, tore open the straw mattresses, and broke anything that happened to be in his path. Within five minutes, the cave looked like Sodom and Amorah after their destruction.

"Chief, maybe we should search outside for the opening of the shaft. The kids will have to come out somewhere, won't they? We'll wait for them and catch them on their way out."

"Why didn't you suggest that sooner, you idiot!" Pelagios was so furious he almost threw the model of the Beis HaMikdash in the poor officer's face.

"I tried, but you wouldn't listen..."

They went outside, but it was too late. Covered in black soot, Yossi and Reuven had already exited the other end of the shaft and started to zigzag between the trees as fast as they could. They were heading for the top of the mountain, to find their friends and warn them about the impending danger.

Chapter Nine

Moon Watching

The orange sun glinted off thousands of helmets that reflected a blinding glare. In the army barracks, rows and rows of daring warriors stood motionless at attention, listening to a speech from Philippos, the Greek ruler.

"Tomorrow at dawn, we'll head out in the direction of Mount Moda'is, in the area of Modi'in.[1] That's where Matisyahu the son of Yochanan lives. According to the information we've received from our most reliable sources, he has been assembling an army, which has already reached about a hundred and fifty soldiers. Their aim? Rebellion!

"We must not waste any time!" Philippos's voice rose a notch. "More Jews are joining his forces every day! True, as of now his men are mostly the weak and elderly, but if the rebellion is not quashed immediately, we could find ourselves with a real problem on our hands. So here's what we're going to do. We'll launch a surprise invasion on their village, and you'll take it from there. You'll make sure that no Jew will even dream of rebellion for the next one hundred years," he said, grinning wickedly.

---

1. *Yosiphon* 20.

The soldiers saluted and left to continue their training exercises. They wanted to be in top form tomorrow.

*   *   *

The group of children and their *rebbi* settled themselves on the mountain peak. The sun was starting to set and they gazed transfixed at the breathtaking sight. From their vantage point on the mountain, they had a wide field of vision, and the fiery red sun, slowly dipping between the pinkish clouds, was awe-inspiring to watch.

"*Mah rabu ma'asecha Hashem*! How great are Your works, Hashem!"[2] cried Elkanah in wonder.

A cool breeze whipped across their faces and sent chills up their spines. Elkanah shivered slightly. He was filled with an inexplicable sense of foreboding, which he quickly brushed away. "I hope everything is okay with Yossi and Reuven," he murmured to himself.

"Rebbi, when will we see the moon?" Yedidya's voice broke into his thoughts.

"Right after sunset we'll start to look for it. Until then, there's no chance that we'll find it. The sun is too bright. We'll return to the cave as soon as we see the moon, if it even appears. I don't want to be here after dark; it's too dangerous."

"Hey, who's that over there?" cried Yehudah nervously, kicking aside a rock that was under his foot.

From a distance of about three hundred feet, they could see two dark figures climbing. The children quickly dropped to the ground.

"You can get up, boys," their *rebbi* informed them after a careful check. "They're Jews just like us."

---

2. *Tehillim* 104:24.

"I wonder what they're looking for here," Mahalalel said. He followed his *rebbi*, who was heading in the direction of the strangers. The rest of the children sat down on the soft grass that grew on the mountaintop.

Elkanah and Mahalalel caught up with the two men. "*Shalom aleichem*," Elkanah greeted them. He looked carefully at the taller of the two; there was something familiar about him.

"*Aleichem shalom*," they replied. "What is a Jew doing with a group of children in the middle of the forest, two hours away from Yerushalayim?"

"We've been living in a cave nearby for the past six months, learning Torah in secret. Occasionally, we come out to see the world and get some fresh air. Today I came to show the boys the new moon."

"That's exactly why we've come," said the shorter man, who hadn't said a word until now.

Elkanah's eyes widened in surprise. "Is *Beis Din* somewhere in this area?"

"Absolutely. The judges are sitting in a secret cave two minutes away from here. With Hashem's help, we will be the witnesses this month."

He tugged lightly on Elkanah's arm, drawing his attention to a specific spot at the foot of the mountain. "Do you see that group of Jews there with the horses? It's hard to see them with all the trees. As soon as *Beis Din* declares Rosh Chodesh, they'll go spread the news throughout the country."

4:40 P.M.

Yossi and Reuven broke out in a frantic run, huffing and puffing. They raced up the mountain, stopping every so often to listen for sounds of their pursuers. After ten minutes of running, they flopped onto the ground, breathing heavily and barely able to speak.

"I...think...we...went...far...enough," said Reuven between deep breaths. "Let's rest...then we'll...look for...our *rebbi*."

Yossi agreed wordlessly. His headache was back, worse than before, and he was feeling awful.

*   *   *

The atmosphere inside the cave was explosive. The officers didn't know what to do with themselves. They went outside and poked through the bushes, looking for the exit of the shaft. They knew fully well that the opening would be concealed behind a mass of forest growth.

Pelagios was left alone inside the cave, angry and irritable. He clutched tightly at the new miniature of the Beis HaMikdash. The officers were all outside, afraid to come in and face their commander. Experience had taught them that when he was angry, he was not a nice person — oh no, not at all. They also knew that he always blamed his failures on other people and none of them wanted to be that other person. That's how thirty husky officers found themselves crawling on the ground outside the cave, searching for the shaft's secret opening.

Fifteen minutes of intensive searching finally produced the desired result: the opening of the tunnel was discovered, so cleverly hidden that even after they found it they could hardly believe it was there.

At the sound of their cries, the chief left the cave to examine their discovery up close. The sky was turning a deep purple hue and a cold wind bit at the nape of Pelagios's neck.

"We're going back to Yerushalayim," he suddenly announced to his men. "You'll soon receive instructions regarding the next stage of our searches."

The chief, used to all his creature comforts, had no interest in staying outside in the middle of the forest on a cold winter night. Grouchy and humiliated, he mounted his horse, sticking the miniature into his bag.

"We're not finished yet," he hissed, urging his horse onward and ignoring the officers who were dragging their feet behind him. "We'll meet again in the next round, and you'll see who the winner will be!"

After a while, neither he nor any of the other officers noticed a figure slip away from the group and backtrack to the cave. Augustus, the chief's Hellenistic assistant, silently returned to the cave alone.

4:42 P.M. SUNSET.

The enormous orange ball of fire slowly disappeared, leaving a trail of crimson-colored clouds in its wake. Elkanah remembered the halachah that one who sees the new moon must go testify, in case one of the other witnesses is disqualified.[3]

"Who knows?" he wondered, gazing at the darkening sky. "Maybe they'll need my testimony."

Some distance from him stood the two other men, searching for the moon in the place they anticipated that it would appear based on their calculations. The moon, though, was nowhere to be seen. In the spot where they expected it to be, there was a medium-sized cloud. A west wind blew, and the cloud moved east.

"It's moving! It's moving!" the boys whispered loudly, a habit they had acquired over the past half a year.

"Soon we'll see the moon!" added a high, excited voice.

One of the witnesses turned his head sharply. That voice was familiar to him.

"Naftali!"

"Abba?"

"Is that you, my Naftali? Is it really you?" his father whispered over and again, hugging his son tightly. They saw nothing

---

3. *Rosh Hashanah* 22a.

around them, not even the moon that suddenly appeared in full glory. A thin, long, sliver was clearly visible in the sky, illuminated in a yellowish-orange light.

It was visible for no more than ten seconds before a cloud began to cover it again.

The children's cries of excitement woke Naftali's father from his

It was visible for no more than ten seconds before a cloud began to cover it again.

reverie. He lifted his tear-filled eyes to the heavens, and a look of disappointment and concern crossed his face. The moon was gone!

"We won't be able to sanctify the new month!"

"Why not? Of course we can! I'll be the second witness," Elkanah volunteered with a broad smile.

The shorter man brought them all back to reality. "We'd better hurry over to *Beis Din* so that we can testify before dark."

"The halachah is that we don't sanctify the new moon at night,"[4] explained Elkanah as they all walked the short distance to the cave. "That's why we try our best to sanctify it before *tzeis hakochavim* of the thirtieth. If the witnesses don't make it on time and three stars appear, then they testify the next day, and only then is Rosh Chodesh declared."[5]

*   *   *

Single-file, the three adults and ten children entered a hole on the side of the mountain. They opened their eyes as wide as they could, trying to adjust to the darkness. It was a medium-sized cave, with one open space in front, almost like a foyer, off of which there was a rocky hallway that led to a spacious inner room where the *dayanim* sat.

From their seat on a felled tree trunk, the *dayanim* stared in amazement at the uninvited group that had just entered. When they heard that Elkanah was the second witness, they instructed him to leave until they finished taking testimony from the first witness.[6]

Outside, Elkanah sat on a wide, comfortable rock and looked around at the forest scenery before him. A slight movement between the trees caught his attention. He jumped up instantly, filled with tension. A few seconds later, two small heads poked

---

4. *Rosh Hashanah* 25b.

5. Rambam, *Hilchos Kiddush HaChodesh* 2:9.

6. *Rosh Hashanah* 23b.

through the brush. Elkanah stared at them, disbelieving.

"We looked for you for a long time!" Reuven's accusatory tone seemed real enough; it couldn't just be Elkanah's imagination. Yes, it was Reuven, and Yossi too.

"What are you doing here? How did you get here?" He didn't like the look of the boys' faces and clothes covered with soot.

All the strain and fear of the past hour burst out in the form of hysterical sobbing. Now Elkanah was really worried.

After a few attempts to calm them, the whole story came pouring out. "What a miracle! What a miracle!" Elkanah kept exclaiming. He couldn't get over the incredible Divine providence that they had all experienced. "If we hadn't gone out to see the moon, we would all be in Greek hands right now!"

"Wait for me here," he instructed the boys, who had gradually relaxed. "The members of *Beis Din* are sitting inside. I'm going into the cave now to testify that I saw the moon, and I don't want to make a ruckus in there. Every minute is precious. If we don't hurry, we'll miss our chance for *kiddush ha-chodesh* today."

Elkanah stood facing the judges and smoothed out his cloak. The eldest of the judges began, "Did you intend to see the moon?"

"Yes. I thought perhaps my testimony would be needed."

"Tell me, was the concave, dark side of the moon facing the sun?"

"No, the rounded, illuminated side was facing the direction of the sun." [7]

"Was the moon to the north or to the south?"

"To the north," answered Elkanah after some thought.

The judges knew that the answer was correct. In the winter months, the moon was visible further north.[8]

"In which direction were its points facing?"

"To the north."

---

7. Ibid., 23b.
8. Ibid., 24a.

"How high in the sky was it?" questioned the judge.

"How high in the sky was it?" questioned the judge.

The children raised eyebrows in surprise. They didn't understand most of the questions, but they kept quiet out of respect. That night, when they were back in the cave, they would ask their *rebbi* to explain everything.

They had no idea that they would not be returning to the cave that night or any other night.

"It was two stories high," they heard their *rebbi* answer.[9]

The judges deliberated in low voices. The answers were consistent with the answers given by the first witness. The head of the *Beis Din* proclaimed in a jubilant voice, "*Mekudash*! Sanctified!" Then the entire audience, which included the other two *dayanim*, three witnesses and ten children, echoed loudly, "*Mekudash, Mekudash!*"[10]

Waves of quiet joy spread through the dark cave. Once again, they had succeeded in keeping the mitzvah of *kiddush ha-chodesh* with great self-sacrifice, in spite of the decrees and the persecution. A sweet sense of closeness to Hashem filled their very being.

When the excitement had subsided somewhat, Elkanah asked for permission to speak. With his shocked students looking on, he told the judges everything he had heard from Yossi and Reuven, who had joined them in the cave in the meantime.

"Now I don't know what to do," he said. "We can't return to the cave, but spending the night outside is dangerous and not an option," he finished off.

The *dayanim* contemplated the situation with the utmost seriousness. "In a case like this, we can't stay here, either. We must leave the area at once," ruled the *av beis din*.

"I live not far from here, in Mount Moda'is," said the second

---

9. Rambam, *Hilchos Kiddush HaChodesh* 2:5.
10. *Rosh Hashanah* 24a.

judge thoughtfully. "It's about an hour's ride, not more. My house has a large attic. I suggest that you come with me and take shelter in the attic temporarily, until we can find a better arrangement for you."

Elkanah's eyes lit up. "*Yasher koach*! That's a very generous offer. But...how will we get there?"

"I have an idea for that, too. Close to this cave there are twenty-five horseback riders waiting. Their job is to spread the news about *kiddush ha-chodesh*. Each child can travel with one rider, who will pass by Mount Moda'is on the way to his destination."

The boys, with the gracious help of the riders, mounted the horses and grabbed tight to the rider's back. Within five minutes, all was quiet again in the region.

Galloping confidently into the darkness, the horses made their way to Mount Moda'is. Elkanah allowed himself to relax. The tension that had gripped him ebbed slightly. Little did he know that he was leading his students straight into the lion's den...

Chapter Ten

Against the Odds

The low, spacious attic was filled with excited commotion. The boys scurried back and forth, carrying straw mattresses, spreading out clean white sheets, and releasing all the stress of the last few hours with laughter and cheerful banter.

The woman of the house did her best to graciously host this group that had suddenly descended on her. She was amazed at the children's strength of character. "So young, and already prepared to give up their lives for Torah!" she kept murmuring.

Up and down, the *dayan* whose house it was climbed the ladder that led to the attic, bringing food and drinks, fresh and dried fruit, clean clothing, and bowls for *netilas yadayim*. Where did he get all these things? The question didn't even occur to the boys, but Elkanah did wonder about it, full of sincere appreciation for the good and generous people who were providing for their needs.

*   *   *

"All your questions will have to wait for tomorrow," Elkanah told Boaz with a tired yawn, when the boy asked him what the judges had meant when they asked about which direction the points of the moon were facing. "I want you all in bed within ten minutes. It's very late already!"

Only after the children had finally fallen asleep, did Elkanah allow himself to acknowledge the extreme exhaustion that had taken hold of him. All the strength seeped out of him at once, and he couldn't stand up a moment longer. The wicker armchair creaked a little when he collapsed into it, totally drained. As if in a dream, the events of the day passed before his eyes, from the time they left the cave, to the testimony about the new moon, to the hurried departure from the forest on horseback. "Tomorrow I'll have to start looking for a new hiding place," he thought wearily. "When will it all be over? For over six months, we've been learning Torah in secret, and there's no end in sight."

Thousands of bright stars twinkled at him through the window. The Beis HaMikdash had been desolate for a long time now. Another Rosh Chodesh had arrived, but no *korban Musaf* could be offered. "How much longer?" He didn't cry out loud, but every bone in his body stiffened at the bitter, pain-filled plea. "Until when will Your strength be in captivity and Your glory in the enemy's hand?"[1] Large tears rolled down his cheeks, as he beseeched Hashem from the depths of his soul. "Arouse Your might and save us, for the sake of Your Name!"

Eyes clenched tight in concentration, his very being was transformed into a prayer as he continued to hum his *tefillah*, until his voice stilled and he fell asleep.

He didn't know it yet, but his prayer had been answered. It wouldn't be long now before salvation came.

*　　　　*　　　　*

In the morning, the boys were able to daven with a *minyan* for the first time in months, and it was a moving sight to see. The pure, sweet sound of their prayer touched the hearts of everyone

---

1. From *Tachanun* recited on Mondays and Thursday.

who heard it. The elated children davened with excitement, answered *Kedushah* and *Barchu*, recited *Chatzi Hallel*[2] with the congregation, and heard the Torah reading for Rosh Chodesh, which mentions the *Musaf* offerings.[3] When mentioning the *korbanos*, they had in mind the principle of *"u'neshalmah farim sefaseinu"*[4] — when it is not possible to actually bring the offerings, we mention them verbally instead.

After a festive breakfast, or to be more precise, a Rosh Chodesh meal, a series of unexpected events quickly unfolded.

The door burst open, and an unfamiliar Jew stood in the entrance. "The watchman has spotted large Greek forces approaching the village!" he blurted out.

Elkanah paled. He was sure that someone had informed on them and now the chief of police was coming to capture them. He rushed the frightened boys up to the attic. Once they were all there, he climbed up last and pulled the ladder up after him. He then gathered them all into a corner of the attic and spoke to them, face flushed with emotion. "Now, during a time of *shmad*, we are commanded not to veer an inch from any of the mitzvos of Hashem. Now, the halachah of *yeihareig v'al ya'avor*, to be killed rather than transgress, applies to every single mitzvah, and even the slightest Jewish custom."[5]

Quietly, he told them what he had heard last night from their host, taking care to leave out the more graphic details. With chills tingling down his spine, he described the heroism of a woman and her seven sons who were caught by the Greek ruler. He ordered them to bow down to an idol, and they refused, going

---

2. *Ta'anis* 28b.

3. *Bemidbar* 28:1–15.

4. *Hoshea* 14:3.

5. Rambam, *Hilchos Yesodei HaTorah* 5:3.

proudly to their deaths. Even the youngest son could not be persuaded to bow down. All seven sons bravely sanctified Hashem's Name and were killed *al kiddush HaShem*.[6]

"Are you prepared to give up your lives *al kiddush HaShem*?" Elkanah asked the boys, looking them straight in the eye.

"Yes!" cried the children in unison, with pure, simple faith. "We will stand strong in the face of every challenge that comes our way! We won't transgress even the smallest detail of the holy Torah."

*   *   *

Matisyahu the Kohen knew the truth. He knew that the approaching armed forces were aimed at him. He knew they would come at some point, but he didn't think it would be so soon. Matisyahu and his sons hadn't had enough time to get organized. Many of the rebels still hadn't arrived at Mount Moda'is, their gathering point, and the weapons in their possession were few and unsophisticated. But they weren't afraid. Matisyahu and his sons reminded themselves and all their fighters, "'These trust in chariots and these in horses, but we mention the Name of Hashem our God.'[7] Let's trust in HaKadosh Baruch Hu and believe that He can save us!"

Together, from the depths of their hearts, they prayed that they would witness the fulfillment of the next *pasuk*: "They kneel and fall, but we rise and gain strength."

*   *   *

The atmosphere in the attic was exalted. The boys listened to Elkanah their *rebbi* more intently than ever before.

---

6. *Yosiphon* 19.

7. *Tehillim* 20:8–9.

"'The voice is the voice of Yaakov, and the hands are the hands of Eisav,'"[8] said their *rebbi*. Only the sound of the children's quiet breathing could be heard. "Our nation's strength is in its mouth. What did our forefathers do in times of trouble? They davened to Hashem, and Hashem heard their prayers and helped them. 'They cried out and Hashem heard, and He saved them from all their troubles.'[9] Come, my precious *talmidim*, let us follow in our ancestors' footstep. Hashem loves *tefillos*, especially the *tefillos* of Jewish children, who are free of sin. Together, we'll say *Tehillim, perek* 22, the *perek* that Queen Esther said when, in her great distress, she came before King Achashveirosh."[10]

"For the musician, on the *ayeles hashachar*, a song of Dovid. My God, my God, why have You forsaken me?"

Elkanah recited the *perek* by heart, and the children repeated after him, *pasuk* by *pasuk*, pleading and crying.

"Save my soul from the sword, my very spirit from the clutches of the dog." [11]

The children's cries arose from the deepest place in their heart, going higher and higher, breaking through all barriers and reaching the heavens.

*   *   *

The low mountain on which Moda'is was situated was surrounded by soldiers. A sea of helmets, shining like the morning sun, was visible from every direction. The Greeks surrounded the

---

8. *Bereishis* 27:22.
9. *Tehillim* 34:18.
10. *Megillah* 15b.
11. *Tehillim* 22:21.

mountain on all sides, careful not to leave the rebels any avenue of escape. Thousands of hulking, well-fed soldiers were equipped with the best weapons. They faced about two hundred Jews, middle-aged and weak, armed with outdated weapons.[12]

In the center, amidst the mass of Greek soldiers, was a fire burning atop an altar. This was an altar for idol worship, built a short time before by the *misyavnim*.

The commander of the brigade hoped that Matisyahu and his men would surrender. "Surrender" meant that Matisyahu would give in and agree to the Greeks' demands, which would serve the Greeks' purposes and encourage other Jews to surrender as well. "If the righteous Matisyahu decided to give up on Torah and mitzvos, there's no reason for us to be stubborn any longer," the Jews would all say to themselves.

The booming voice of the Greek crier echoed in the air. "Listen here, Matisyahu the Kohen! You are a respected man among your people. Obey the command of King Antiochus and you will live and not die!"

Matisyahu did not budge. Without batting an eyelash and without flinching, he courageously gave his unequivocal answer. "I will obey the command of **my** King, and you will obey the command of your king as he has instructed you!"

The commander was beginning to understand that Matisyahu was not going to deliver the "goods." He would rather die than surrender. Thousands of soldiers stood silently, waiting for the signal. Before the commander could decide what to do next, a Hellenistic Jew stepped out from the ranks of Greek soldiers.

"I am very surprised at the behavior of the King's agents and his army," he cried loudly. "How can you stand by and allow Matisyahu to brazenly ignore His Majesty's orders?"

---

12. *Yosiphon* 20.

The booming voice of the Greek crier echoed in the air.

The *misyavein* grabbed a pig that stood nearby, drew his sword and chopped off the animal's head. He waved the carcass around and then threw it into the fire on the altar of the *avodah zarah*.

For a moment, there was utter silence. The only sound was the crackle of the flames licking at the meat.

Then, like the rumble of thunder, came the sound of stomping feet.

The sight of a Jew sacrificing a pig for idol worship had spurred Matisyahu to action. He couldn't restrain himself any longer. With the speed of a youngster, he ran over to the altar, brandished his sword, and before anyone knew what was happening he killed the *misyavein*. The soldiers still hadn't had a chance to react when Matisyahu leapt out like an arrow and killed the Greek commander.

The great revolt had begun! With cries of "Salvation is Hashem's!"[13] Matisyahu's sons and the other rebels raced down the mountain, while the bewildered Greeks scattered in fear. Thousands of Greek fighters broke out in a frenzied run, with the Jews right behind, killing them as they went. The first battle ended with a decisive victory for the Jews.

> **"You championed their cause, defended their rights, and avenged their wrong. You delivered the strong into the hands of the weak, the many into the hands of the few, the impure into the hands of the pure, the wicked into the hands of the righteous, and the wanton sinners into the hands of those who study Your Torah."[14]**

*　　　　　*　　　　　*

---

13. *Tehillim* 3:9.
14. *Tefillas Al HaNissim.*

The sounds of battle were carried by the wind and reached the crowded attic. The children huddled together, and their piercing *tefillos* reached the heavens. They had no doubt that in a few more seconds, or minutes at most, the Greeks would burst in on them.

"Rebbi didn't tell us what *berachah* we're supposed to make!" Zevulun was panicky. His voice shook as he spoke and he leaned on Elkanah, trying to draw strength and encouragement.

"*Berachah*? On what?" His friends thought that all the stress was causing him to say gibberish.

"On the mitzvah of *kiddush HaShem*," Zevulun yelled, his face reddening.

Elkanah answered in a clear, quiet voice. "*Baruch Ata Hashem Elokeinu Melech ha-olam, asher kideshanu b'mitzvosav v'tzivanu l'kadesh Shemo ba'rabim.*[15] That's the *berachah*. But before we say it, let us do *teshuvah*." Elkanah opened his *Tehillim* to *perek* 51, the *mizmor* of *teshuvah*. Sobbing, the children repeated after him:

"Create for me a pure heart, Hashem, and renew a steadfast spirit within me. Do not cast me away from before You, and do not take Your holy spirit from me."[16]

They wanted to go to their deaths pure and cleansed of sin. The seconds seemed to drag on for an eternity. When the last words of the *perek* crossed their lips, they suddenly heard their host's voice from downstairs.

"A miracle! Boys! It's a great miracle!" he yelled, tripping over his words in his excitement. "They ran away! The Greeks ran for their lives!"

Elkanah ran to the entrance of the attic, a look of disbelief on his face.

---

15. Shelah HaKadosh, *Sha'ar HaOsios, aleph.*
16. *Tehillim* 51:12–13.

"Yes, yes! It's true!" the *dayan* insisted. "You can come out now! We've been saved!"

Wordlessly, Elkanah turned and went back to the children. This time, he opened his *Tehillim* to *perek* 136, and together with his *talmidim* he recited the words fervently, with overwhelming gratitude to Hashem.

> **"*Hodu la-Shem ki tov, ki l'olam chasdo*! Give thanks to Hashem because He is good, for His kindness is forever. Give thanks to the God of the mighty, for His kindness is forever... Who remembered us in our humbled state, for His kindness is forever. And He rescued us from our enemies, for His kindness is forever."** [17]

By nightfall, the village was still abuzz. The Jews couldn't get over the wonder of it all. The dramatic shift from the morning's sheer terror to the intense relief that followed was electrifying. They kept rehashing the day's events, retelling the miracles Hashem had performed for them.

"I stood nearly emptyhanded facing a big, muscular Greek with armor from head to toe. I waved my shepherd's staff at him and he turned and ran away like a scared rabbit," a short, scrawny Jew said, tugging at his beard in amazement.

"When I ran down the mountain, I noticed a group of Greek soldiers who were so confused that they were fighting against each other," his friend said, a grateful smile plastered across his face.

"And listen to the miracle that happened to me!" added a Jew with a dark beard and *peyos* and flaming black eyes. "The Greek who was standing opposite me wanted to draw his sword, but all that came out of the sheath was the handle. The blade got stuck

17. *Tehillim* 136:1–2, 23–24.

inside! 'It's witchcraft!' he started to yell. 'This Jew is casting a spell on me!' Then he fell to the ground in a faint."

"It's a miracle! An unbelievable miracle! A handful of poorly armed and untrained Jews defeated an army of thousands of skilled fighters!"

"The truth? I was scared to join Matisyahu's army," another Jew confessed. "I was sure they would fail. How could I have been so foolish? They're fighting for Hashem! Of course Hashem is going to fight for them!"

Matisyahu himself did not take part in the celebration. He sat at home with his five sons, and together they planned their next move. After much deliberation and thought, they reached a decision. "First of all, tomorrow morning our men will go out on a *bris milah* campaign, to circumcise babies throughout the region.[18] That will be a great *zechus* for *Klal Yisrael*, the same way our ancestors performed the mitzvah of *bris milah* before they left Egypt, in order to gain merit. Second, we will go up to Yerushalayim, purify the city and renew the *avodah* in the Beis HaMikdash. Third, once Yerushalayim is in our hands, we will continue to fight until the last Greek leaves our Land." Exhausted yet fulfilled, the Maccabim went to rest a bit before dawn.

All night long, a steady stream of Jews made their way to Mount Moda'is. Those who feared Hashem, who heard about the day's miracles, hurried to join Matisyahu's army. Over the next few days, the news spread throughout the country and the small band of fighters grew in number.

Thousands of Jews, guardians of tradition, fearlessly began to keep the mitzvos in public again. Within a week, the rebels had organized themselves into a well-ordered army, and the signal was given to go up to Yerushalayim.

---

18. *Yosiphon* 20.

Chapter Eleven

Return of Augustus

Augustus the *misyavein*, the police chief's assistant, was by nature a gentle, thoughtful person, but unfortunately he had grown up in a Tzedoki home. In his parents' house, only the mitzvos stated explicitly in the Written Torah were observed, and even these were only performed to the best of their understanding and not according to the traditions passed down from the days of Moshe Rabbeinu. When the Greeks came to Eretz Yisrael, bringing with them winds of "enlightenment" and "progress," Augustus joined them willingly. His parents did not object to his decision, and he himself, despite his distaste for the Greeks' cruel, coercive methods, welcomed the opportunities for sports and art that were now offered to him.

Augustus was an outstanding student. His teachers appreciated his many talents and appointed him the personal assistant of Pelagios, the Greek police chief in Yerushalayim. Augustus served the chief with great devotion, and his boss was very pleased with him. Life was good for Augustus, until the episode of the house takeover, which showed him his master's true colors.

It all started because Pelagios was unhappy with the small house he lived in and decided to look for more spacious quarters. He went to look at every house that was up for sale, but nothing met his demands. On one of his house-hunting expeditions, though, he saw the home of Binyamin, Reuven's father, and decided that it was perfect for him.

Without even the slightest misgivings, he forged a letter from the Greek court in Yaffo. This falsified document accused Binyamin of delivering classes on the laws of Shabbos to dozens of Jews. The letter decreed that as a punishment for his crime he was to be sold into slavery. The letter also said that the chief of police in Yerushalayim was responsible for carrying out the sentence.

*   *   *

It was a quiet afternoon and Binyamin sat in his room learning. The children played happily in the spacious foyer, when suddenly the door burst open and there stood a squadron of officers and their commander.

"Where is your father?" The chief looked at them with cold eyes, and an evil, heartless grin crossed his face.

The children's frightened cries brought Binyamin running, and his eyes widened in horror when he saw the officers.

"You're coming with us," said a tall officer as he chained Binyamin's hands. "And don't waste your words arguing," he added, when he saw Binyamin opening his mouth in defense. "The sentence is final, signed by the highest authorities. There's nothing to talk about."

Binyamin was taken and sold as a slave to a Lebanese timber merchant. His house was confiscated, and of course ownership was transferred to the police chief. The cries and screams of Binyamin's family fell on deaf ears. Brokenhearted, his wife and children wandered homeless in the street until they found an old abandoned shack to live in.

The cruel eviction from their house, their father's captivity, and the stark contrast between their luxurious and spacious home and their current dilapidated residence did not crush their spirits. Binyamin's wife stayed strong, encouraging her children to do the same. She sent Reuven to join the group in the mountains, and at home she kept the daily routine running as much as possible. Only Augustus found it impossible to go back to his daily life. The police chief's terrible corruption shocked him to the core. True, he was not religious and he wasn't particularly fond of religious people, but the contrast between Pelagios's savage behavior and the nobility and strength of character of Binyamin's family struck him very deeply.

That same evening, after Pelagios left for the gambling house, Augustus sneaked into his master's private room and took the money that he had been paid in exchange for Binyamin. "I'll hide this money in a secret place," he thought. "At the earliest opportunity, I'll buy Binyamin's freedom from his Lebanese master."

*   *   *

Ten months passed, and despite Augustus's good intentions, he forgot all about his resolution. The day that he entered Pelagios's room and saw the model of the Beis HaMikdash, he happened to pick it up and turn it over, and the simple inscription on the bottom reminded him of his promise. Later, after chatting with his master, he found out that Pelagios planned to capture Reuven, Binyamin's son, and force him and his friend to study art.

That night, Augustus tossed and turned in bed. Sleep seemed a million miles away. His conscience plagued him. "How could I have forgotten about my plan to release Binyamin from slavery?" he couldn't stop thinking. Shortly before dawn, he fell asleep after promising himself that he would take care of the matter the very next day.

The visit to the cave peeled away another layer from his heart. The conditions, or more precisely, the lack of conditions in which the children of the Perushim lived, stunned him. "Look how these young boys are ready to give up on so many things just to learn Torah," he berated himself, "while you, an adult, cannot forgo even the smallest pleasure. Would you be willing to make such a sacrifice?" He knew that the answer was "no." That was the moment when the first seeds of *teshuvah* sprouted in his heart.

At a certain point, during the march back to Yerushalayim, he slipped away from the group of officers and headed back to the cave. The darkness in the forest was absolute, and for a long time Augustus wandered hopelessly among the trees, trying to find the place.

"I'll sleep outside on the grass tonight and continue on my way in the morning," he decided. In the morning, with the aid of the sun's light, he remembered the right direction. He reached the cave, and, as he expected, it was empty. Daylight filtered inside and colored the stone walls an array of pastel hues. The light illuminated a small object hidden on a stone shelf in the corner. Augustus slowly approached, and with trembling hands he lifted Elkanah's tefillin and hugged them to his heart.

"*Avinu Malkeinu, hachazireinu bi'seshuvah sheleimah lefanecha*! I want to return to you, Hashem!" His cries bounced off the walls of the cave and echoed back at him a thousand times. "My Father in heaven! I know I've strayed so far, but I'm still Your son! Help me, Father! I want to come back!"

Trembling, he withdrew the holy black boxes from their case. "You dirty sinner! You eater of *treif* meat and non-kosher food!" sneered his inner voice. "How dare you touch these holy objects?"

White-faced, he put down the tefillin. "I'll immerse in the pool of water here in the cave, and then I'll put on the tefillin," he told himself.

After emerging from the water, he felt purer. He wrapped himself in a tallis, put on the tefillin, and began to pour out his heart to his Creator. His *tefillah* went on for three hours. The silent cave walls stared in amazement at the river of tears that fell from his eyes. For the first time in his life, he really davened, begging and pleading for Hashem's forgiveness. When he finished, he felt a sense of belonging and closeness to Hashem that he had never experienced before. He knew what he had to do now.

He wrapped himself in a tallis, put on the tefillin,
and began to pour out his heart to his Creator.

"I'm never going to work for Pelagios again. I'm going straight to Lebanon, to do whatever I can to release Binyamin from slavery."

*   *   *

The army of the Chashmonaim slowly advanced in the direction of Yerushalayim, its ranks swelling every day. More and more fighters joined the cause, strengthening their parched souls in the process. The fight was almost secondary. This army's main goal was to spread Torah and mitzvos, eradicate idol worship, and open up the locked *batei knesses* and *batei midrash*.

The Greek army couldn't stop them. With a helplessness they hadn't experienced in years, the Greeks sent an urgent call to Syria for assistance and waited impatiently for the reinforcements they were promised.

*   *   *

From the royal palace in Syria, King Antiochus followed the latest development with outrage. The Jews' impudence and boldness made his blood boil. At first he mocked their attempt at rebellion, which he viewed as a little local uprising doomed to failure. But the reports that reached him now were getting progressively worse and he was more than a little worried. The rebels had advanced, conquering more and more territory along the way.

"The Jewish rebels are on their way to Yerushalayim," his adjutant informed him that morning.

It was the straw that broke the camel's back.

"Insubordinates!" roared Antiochus. "Just you wait! In a few more days, you'll be crushed like ants. Rusmus, inform the ministers and generals that at exactly one o'clock this afternoon there will be an emergency meeting and no lateness will be tolerated!"

The meeting was long and stormy. One of the ministers suggested a mass campaign to kill all the Jews in Eretz Yisrael. The suggestion was rejected by a majority of votes, with the Minister of Higher Education reasonably stating that the war against the Jews was a war of the spirit and not the body.

"This is a matter of principle," argued the Minister of Higher Education. "Is there one God, as the Jews believe, or many gods, as we claim? Which is the true wisdom — the wisdom of the Torah or Greek wisdom? We will not achieve our goal by killing out the Jews. Our goal will be accomplished only when we succeed in getting all the Jews to deny the truth of Torah!"

At the end of the meeting, the adjutant announced the final decision in a nasal voice. "An army of eighty thousands soldiers, under the command of Lysandros, will be sent to Eretz Yisrael. Its mission: to restore Eretz Yisrael to Greek control. Once the land is conquered, we will continue to exert heavy pressure on the Jews to abandon their religion."

The adjutant cleared his throat and banged his gavel on the ornate wooden table. "In the name of His Majesty the King, this meeting is hereby adjourned."

*　　　　*　　　　*

"In the meantime, we're staying here," Elkanah pinched Boaz's cheek and smiled faintly. "It's the best option we have right now."

Their learning sessions took place in the local *beis midrash*, where three of the village boys joined them as well. Meals were provided by their host, the *dayan*, and they slept in the attic.

Over the next few days, getting the children to concentrate on their studies became an almost impossible mission. News from the battlefield streamed in constantly and excited the boys. They were no longer detached from the rest of the world, the way they had been in the cave. They overheard conversations and knew that the Chashmonaim were on the way to Yerushalayim. Their concern for the welfare of their families gave them no rest.

"At a time like this," Elkanah prodded them again and again, "*Klal Yisrael* needs the *zechus* of our Torah learning and *tefillos* more than ever."

Chapter Twelve

Battle Cries

"Everyone knows what role the Kohanim play in the *avodah* in the Beis HaMikdash. The Leviyim have very important jobs, too: they sing, guard, and open the gates.[1] But it seems like the Yisraelim have no part in the *avodah* at all." Naftali stretched out on a bench, waiting for a reply from his *rebbi*.

"Your question is a good one," answered Elkanah. A chill blew in through the arched window and Elkanah got up to close it. "We, the Yisraelim, cannot serve in the Beis HaMikdash by ourselves. That privilege is given only to the tribe of Levi, the only tribe that did not sin with the Golden Calf.[2] Before the Mishkan was built, the job of bringing *korbanos* was entrusted to the firstborns of Bnei Yisrael. After *Cheit HaEigel*, that privilege was taken away from them and transferred to the tribe of Levi.[3]

"Moshe Rabbeinu proclaimed, '*Mi laShem eilay* — Whoever is for Hashem, join me![4] Anyone to whom Hashem's honor is important should join me in punishing the sinners!'

---

1. Rambam, *Hilchos Klei HaMikdash* 3:2.
2. *Devarim* 10:8.
3. *Zevachim* 112b.
4. *Shemos* 32:26.

"All of *shevet* Levi answered that call, and Moshe commanded them to kill those who had sinned."

Yossi raised him hand. "In Moshe's *berachah* to *shevet* Levi it says, 'Who said about the father of his mother, "I did not see my relationship to him," and who didn't recognize his maternal brother or know his grandsons...'[5] That means that the Leviyim even killed their relatives from other tribes who sinned."

"Very nice, Yossi!" Elkanah said in appreciation. "The continuation of the *pasuk* tells us why the Leviyim specifically merited these privileges: "For they kept Your word" — they didn't worship idols, which Hashem clearly forbade with His words in the *Aseres HaDibros*: '*Lo yihiyeh lecha elohim acheirim.*'"[6]

Elkanah stood up and paced in front of the children. "That's why the Leviyim became the teachers of Torah, as it says, '*Yoru mishpatecha l'Yaakov v'sorascha l'Yisrael* — They will teach Your laws to Yaakov, and Your Torah to Israel.'[7] Think about it. How many of the *dayanim* that you know are from the tribe of Levi? And, as we know, the continuation of the *berachah* is: '*Yasimu ketorah b'apecha v'chalil al mizbechecha* — They will place incense before You and burnt offerings on Your *Mizbeach*.' The children of Aharon were given the privilege of doing the *avodah* in the Beis HaMikdash.

"What I never understood until recently, though, is the last part of Moshe's *berachah* to Levi: '*Mechatz masnayim kamav u'mesanav min yekumun* — Crush the loins of those who rise up against him and his enemies, so that they will not rise.'[8] Up until now, we never heard about any wars initiated by the tribe of Levi! But

5. *Devarim* 33:9.
6. Rashi, ibid.
7. *Devarim* 33:10.
8. Ibid., 33:11.

over the last week the answer has become clear to me." Elkanah paused and smiled at his students.

"The Chashmonaim!" cried Boaz excitedly. Two Jews learning nearby turned around to look at him. Boaz blushed and lowered his voice. "Matisyahu and his sons are Kohanim, from the tribe of Levi!"[9]

"Their success in this impossible battle against the Greeks comes from the blessing they received from Moshe Rabbeinu," Elkanah added. "See how important the self-sacrifice of Levi is in the eyes of Hashem! Many years ago, they stood as one and rallied to Moshe's cry of 'Mi laShem eilay.' Now, more than a thousand years later, we are still reaping the benefits of that act!"

Elkanah fingered the scratched-up table and whispered passionately, "Today, as well, anyone who cares about Hashem's honor and goes out to fight Hashem's battle, will receive a reward for himself and his children for all generations."[10]

"Maybe we should join the fighters. We also want to take part in the war and get rewarded," suggested Yedidya, half-kidding, half-serious.

Elkanah's expression was thoughtful. "If Hashem wanted you to go out and fight, you would have been born a few years earlier, so that today you'd be old enough to participate in the battle. What Hashem wants from you now is to serve Him in the battle of Torah learning."

The air was hot and stuffy by then, and Elkanah went to open the window, peering out for a moment at the sandy hills that spread as far as the horizon. "The Torah equates the reward of those who stay behind and guard the camp with the reward of those who go out to fight.[11] Why? Because in wartime, the fighters

---

9. Rashi, ibid.

10. The Chofetz Chaim related this idea to the people of his generation, as well.

11. Rashi, *Bereishis* 14:24.

cannot be victorious if the guards don't do their job. We have to fulfill our role in Torah and *tefillah*, and that will enable the fighters to win the war."

Reuven opened his mouth hesitantly. A barely perceptible nod from Elkanah encouraged him to speak up.

"But...but...at least Rebbi should go out to fight!" he stammered uncomfortably, finding it hard to express himself.

"I am taking a very important part in this war and it is something I must continue to do. I'm learning with you! If I stop doing that, *Klal Yisrael* might suffer defeat! During the conquest of Eretz Yisrael, an angel came to Yehoshua and berated him for neglecting his Torah learning! Yehoshua immediately strengthened himself in this area, and later, even when they lay siege, he spent the whole night learning Torah in order to fulfill the instructions of the angel who came to tell him that without Torah the Jewish people have no chance of winning."[12]

"Rebbi, this is really fascinating!" Naftali absently rearranged the simple linen tablecloth that covered the wooden table and waved one hand aside in a questioning motion. "But I still didn't get an answer to my question. What is the role of the other tribes in the Beis HaMikdash?"

"A Yisrael can slaughter a *korban*,"[13] Yossi offered helpfully.

"That is uncommon with a *korban tzibbur*, because the Kohanim of the *mishmeres* hold a lottery to divvy up all the jobs, including *shechitah*," said Elkanah. "But an individual who brings a *korban* can slaughter it himself, and the Kohanim are not allowed to withhold that privilege from him."[14]

---

12. *Megillah* 3a.

13. *Berachos* 31b.

14. *Chomer BaKodesh* (introduction of the *Tiferes Yisrael* to *Seder Kodashim*) 1:2.

"A non-Kohen can also skin the animal and cut it up!"[15] added Reuven.

Elkanah agreed with him and added another detail. "Only a Yisrael whose lineage is known[16] may skin and cut up the *korbanos*.[17] But aside from slaughtering, skinning and cutting up the animal, the Yisraelim have another very important role in the *avodah* of the *korbanos*," Elkanah said.

The boys opened their eyes wide in surprise and tried to think what it might be.

"They give *machatzis ha-shekel*, and the *korbanos tzibbur* are bought with their money,"[18] guessed Yehudah.

"That's true," the *rebbi* said softly, "but I had something else in mind. Something similar to the type of role we're filling right now."

"Oh, of course!" Mahalalel remembered. "*Anshei ma'amad*! My father is the head of one of the *mishmaros* of the *anshei ma'amad*!"

"*Anshei ma'amad*!" the boys all chorused after him. "How could we have forgotten?"

They were familiar with the concept and listened with interest as their *rebbi* explained the reason for this job. "Regarding the *korban Tamid*, the Torah says, 'You shall watch over My offering and My food that is put on the fire of my *Mizbeach*, as a pleasing aroma before Me, to offer to Me at its appointed time.'[19] For every *korban* that is brought, the owner has to stand there while it is being offered. However, when it comes to *korbanos tzibbur*, there's a problem. The owner of the *korban* is the entirety of *Klal*

---

15. Rambam, *Hilchos Bi'as HaMikdash* 9:6.
16. *Tosfos, Kiddushin* 76b, s.v. *ayn*.
17. *Tosfos, Kesubos* 24b, s.v. *chad amar*.
18. Rashi, *Shemos* 30:15.
19. *Bemidbar* 28:2.

Yisrael! How can this *korban* be offered *l'chatchilah* if the owner, *Klal Yisrael*, is not standing there?"

"It's impossible for all the Jews who contributed *machatzis ha-shekel* to stand in the Beis HaMikdash every morning!" argued Zevulun, brushing away a fly that had landed on his hand.

"Exactly. So in order to fulfill this halachah as much as possible, a system of shifts was set up. The shifts, called *mishmaros anshei ma'amad*, act as representatives of *Am Yisrael* while the *korbanos tzibbur* are being offered."[20]

"I get it! *Ma'amad* is from the word '*omdim*,' standing, because they stand 'to watch' over the offering during the bringing of the *korbanos*," added Boaz, who had a knack for language and grammar.

"Who was chosen to be the *anshei ma'amad*?" Reuven asked with interest.

Elkanah sat down and explained. "The same way there are twenty-four *mishmaros*, shifts, of Kohanim, and every week a different *mishmeres* serves in the Beis HaMikdash, so too the *anshei ma'amad* are divided into twenty-four shifts. Part of every *ma'amad* is made up of residents of Yerushalayim, while the other part consists of Jews living in other cities in Eretz Yisrael. When the turn of their *mishmeres* comes, the members of the *ma'amad* who live in or near Yerushalayim go to the Beis HaMikdash to stand there while the *korbanos* are being offered. Those who live far away gather in the city of the head of the *ma'amad* and daven that the *korbanos* should be accepted."[21]

"But who gets the *zechus* of being the *anshei ma'amad*?" Reuven repeated his question. In his mind's eyes, he could already see himself as one of them…

---

20. *Ta'anis* 26a.
21. *Ta'anis* 27a.

"The *anshei ma'amad* are worthy Jews who fear sin.[22] They also fast four days during the week of their *mishmeres*, from Monday to Thursday, eating only at night."[23]

"Why don't they fast on Sunday?"

"One of the reasons is that after a restful Shabbos comes Sunday, when the work and toil of the week begins. The transition from rest to work makes fasting difficult."[24]

"But they don't fast on Friday either!"

"That's so they won't go into Shabbos fasting, and also because they need their strength to prepare for Shabbos."

Yehudah suddenly jumped up in place, knocking over the bench with a loud clatter. "I heard that they also daven an extra *tefillah* every day. Is that true?" he asked, bending over to pick up the bench.

"Absolutely," confirmed Elkanah, reaching out to help him. "In addition to all the usual *tefillos*, they also daven the Yom Kippur *Ne'ilah*, and they read the story of Creation from the Torah."[25]

"They read from *Parshas Bereishis*? Why?"

"There is a very close connection between the *korbanos* and the creation of the world. Without *korbanos*, the world cannot exist."[26]

"Oh, when will we be able to bring *korbanos* again?" Yedidya's clear voice rang out, expressing the ache they all felt inside. The curtains covering the windows rustled slightly, as if they too shared his wish.

"Children, it will be very soon." Their *rebbi*'s hushed voice sent chills up their spines. "Just moments before we began our lesson, I received the news. The Chashmonaim are standing at the gates of Yerushalayim!"

---

22. Rambam, *Hilchos Klei HaMikdash* 6:1.
23. *Ta'anis* 27b.
24. Ibid., 26a.
25. Ibid.
26. Ibid., 27b.

Chapter Thirteen

The Wood Offering

Bundled in warm clothing and carrying a large leather sack on his shoulder that contained a money pouch, Augustus made his way north. He still had not changed his style of dress to look like a Jew. Rumor had it that the north was still under Greek control, and the future was unclear. Some of the Greek commanders favored sending forces south to join the battle against the Chashmonaim, while others preferred to wait for reinforcements. The Jews in the northern cities still could not keep mitzvos publicly, but they were no longer so afraid. Greek persecutions were on hold; they were afraid of the Jews' revenge should the Chashmonaim win the war.

At the end of three days' journey, Augustus stepped foot in Tzidon, a large city in Lebanon. He made inquiries here and there and found the timber merchant who had purchased Binyamin as a slave ten months earlier.

Augustus dressed up like a wealthy businessman, combed his hair, and went to the home of Binyamin's master. He introduced himself as a fellow timber merchant and asked to talk business. The master welcomed him in graciously and ushered him into a spacious parlor.

The parlor was luxuriously furnished. Heavy curtains hung from the windows, and comfortable armchairs were positioned around low marble tables.

At the master's summons, a tall man in servant's clothing entered the room and set down a shining tray full of beautiful fruit.

"Who is that?" asked Augustus, his heart pounding furiously.

"That is an especially fine slave," boasted the Lebanese man. "He's from Yerushalayim. I paid a fortune for him, but he was worth it. He has a very strong work ethic and doesn't waste a minute!" He continued singing the slave's praises as if he was describing one of his best trees.

"Maybe you'd like to sell him to me?" asked Augustus in a bored tone, doing his best to conceal his excitement. "I need someone exactly like that to accompany me on business trips."

"How much?" asked the merchant greedily.

"How much what?"

"How much would you pay for him?"

Augustus cautiously named a sum that was slightly less than the amount he had, purposely leaving room for negotiation. The Tzidoni laughed.

"Are you kidding me? I bought him for fifteen hundred gold dinars. He's a smart, hard-working slave, and I won't sell him for less than three thousand dinars!"

Augustus felt the blood drain from his face. Two additional attempts to convince the merchant failed, and he left the house distraught. "It won't be as simple as I thought," he muttered to himself. "I'll have to think of another way. I only have the fifteen hundred gold dinars that I took from Pelagios, plus another five hundred dinars of my own that I saved up over the last year."

*   *   *

In the room he had rented in a simple inn, the former *misyavein* sat and planned his next steps. "First, I'll try to collect money for *pidyon shvuyim*, redeeming a captive," he decided.

He went out to knock on the doors of local Jews but returned to his room disappointed. The local Jews sincerely wanted to help, but most of them were terribly poor and the little they had given him was not enough. The rich ones among them were Tzedokim, who preferred money over mitzvos. Their gold was too precious to them to spend it on helping redeem a fellow Jew.

All night, Augustus tossed and turned on the narrow bed, and when the morning's first light dawned he reached a decision. "Binyamin will have to be smuggled out!"

*   *   *

Four months earlier, an urgent meeting had been held in the home of the Parosh family.

"We must give final approval for a wood shipment from Lebanon, and we still have not reached a decision." The head of the family, from the tribe of Yehudah, looked from his brothers to his sons, waiting for an answer.

"Rosh Chodesh Teves, the time when we bring our *korban eitzim*,[1] is getting closer, and the *avodah* in the Beis HaMikdash has not yet resumed since it was stopped by the Greeks. I think there's no reason to order wood right now," said the youngest of the group.

"No reason?!" cried the middle brother. "Ending a two-hundred-year tradition means nothing to you?"

The oldest brother, Yehudah, closed his eyes wearily. His family's glorious history flashed through his mind.

About two hundred years ago, Ezra and Nechemiah returned to Eretz Yisrael and built the Beis HaMikdash. The Jews in Eretz Yisrael at that time lived in utter poverty. They barely managed to raise funds for building the Beis HaMikdash, *korbanos*, and reconstructing the wall around Yerushalayim, which was an expensive project.

---

1. *Ta'anis* 26a.

When the Beis HaMikdash was complete, a few distinguished Jewish families volunteered to donate the wood for the fire on the *Mizbeach*.[2]

The sons of Arach from the tribe of Yehudah contributed a large amount of wood on the first of Nissan; it was enough to last until the nineteenth of Tammuz. The sons of Dovid from the tribe of Yehudah donated next, and their wood lasted fifteen days, from the twentieth of Tammuz until the fourth of Av. Next, the sons of Parosh brought their donation, but it was only enough wood for two days, the fifth and sixth of Av.[3]

After them, there were other families, a total of eight, who generously provided wood for the *Mizbeach* until the first of Teves. On that day, a lottery was held between them, to determine which families would donate next. The Parosh family got three more months: Teves, Shevat and Adar.[4]

By the next year, the Jews' financial situation had improved, and there was enough money from the *machatzis ha-shekel* collection to buy the wood for the Beis HaMikdash. In appreciation for the families who had helped out during difficult times, the Anshei Knesses HaGedolah decreed that those families would have a special *zechus*: every single year, on the day they had donated wood during the first year of the Second Beis HaMikdash, *korbanos* would be brought and all the wood burning on the *Mizbeach* would be donated by them.[5]

The Parosh family had two days like this: the fifth of Av and the first of Teves.[6] And now, with a wave of his hand, one of the

---

2. Ibid., 28a.

3. Rashi, *Ta'anis* 26a, s.v. *bnei Arach*.

4. *Tosfos Yom Tov*, Mishnah *Ta'anis* 4:5.

5. *Ta'anis* 28a.

6. Ibid., 26a.

brothers was ready to give up this special tradition? The oldest brother contorted his face in pain.

At the end of a long discussion, the family decided to order the wood. "Whenever the *avodah* in the Beis HaMikdash resumes, it will probably take a few days for them to organize enough wood. In the meantime, they'll be able to use our wood and we'll have a mitzvah," the middle son reasoned, and the others agreed.

The family sent a messenger to Tzidon in Lebanon, a city famous for its cedar trees,[7] and closed a deal with Binyamin's master, the wood merchant they always did business with.

Their agreement was carefully drafted and signed. Among other things, the contract stipulated that the two hundred excellent-quality tree trunks the merchant promised to provide would be cut before the fifteenth of Av.[8] Wormy wood is not fit for use on the *Mizbeach*, and wood that was cut before the fifteenth of Av and thoroughly dried out would not be wormy.

In the Beis HaMikdash, in the *Lishkas HaEitzim*(47), Kohanim with blemishes that disqualified them from doing the actual *avodah* were put to work checking the wood for the *Mizbeach*, to make sure it was worm-free.[9]

A deposit changed hands and the deal was sealed. The wood merchant appointed none other than Binyamin to be responsible for sending out the huge wood delivery. This cheered up the Jewish slave and brought a ray of light into the darkness of his captivity. Here he was, preparing wood for the *korbanos* that would soon resume!

Binyamin believed that with all his heart.

---

7. *I Melachim* 5:20.

8. *Ta'anis* 31a.

9. Mishnah *Middos* 2:5.

Here he was, preparing wood for the korbanos that would soon resume!

Chapter Fourteen

Mizbeach under Construction

On the twenty-fifth of Kislev, the Jews overcame the Greeks.[1] After a brief struggle, the Chashmonaim entered the gates of Yerushalayim. On that day, the Jews were delivered from their enemies' hands, and that is one of the reasons for the name "Chanukah": חנו כ"ה, they rested on the twenty-fifth.[2]

Their first stop was the place they had been pining for all these months: the Beis HaMikdash. As they stood on the threshold of this holy place, their joy and excitement was boundless, but very quickly their joy turned into mourning and their excitement turned to horror. The Beis HaMikdash was filled with *tum'ah*. There were Greek idols in every corner of the *Azarah*, and on the holy *Mizbeach* a fire crackled and consumed non-kosher meat.

The Chashmonaim could not allow themselves to sink into despair. They had to purify the Beis HaMikdash as soon as possible. That same day, they set up a *Beis Din* made up of the remaining Sages of the Sanhedrin who still lived in Yerushalayim,

---

1. Rambam, *Hilchos Chanukah* 3:2.
2. Ran, *Shabbos* 21b.

along with the elders of the Kohanim who arrived in the city with the army of the Chashmonaim.

The *Beis Din* convened immediately to discuss a number of relevant halachic questions. The purification of the Beis HaMikdash and reinstatement of the *avodah* of the *korbanos* were the first and most pressing challenges they faced. Matisyahu knew that the Greeks wouldn't leave them alone so fast. There would be a respite of a few weeks while the Greeks regrouped and rearmed, and then they would surely launch a new attack.

"The merit of the *korbanos* will help us defeat the enemy,"[3] thought Matisyahu. "We must resume the *avodah* as soon as we can!"

*   *   *

A number of energetic community leaders banded together and marched through the desecrated city, demolishing the bolts that blocked the entrances of the *batei midrash*, filling them with *sifrei Torah* and *sifrei Nevi'im* and offering the people Torah classes.

The residents lovingly assisted them. The people of Yerushalayim had waited longingly for this moment. Just a few hours after the city was conquered by the Chashmonaim, the sound of Torah learning already reverberated in the streets. Words and *pesukim* hung in the air, sliding down the mountain slopes, carrying the exhilarating news wherever they went: Torah has returned to the city! It was the embodiment of the *pasuk*, "For out of Tzion shall the Torah come forth, and the word of Hashem from Yerushalayim."[4]

*   *   *

---

3. *Otzar HaMidrashim, Vayikra* p. 16.

4. *Yeshayahu* 2:3.

The joyous news spread as if on wings to every city in Eretz Yisrael.

Three hours after the Chashmonaim stepped trough the gates of the city, a messenger came galloping on horseback to the city of Moda'is, breathlessly delivering the news. "Hashem has helped us! Yerushalayim was captured by the Chashmonaim!"

His jubilant cries reached the *beis ha-knesses* where the boys sat and learned. For a moment, they stared at each other in disbelief, and then they burst out in a jumble of excited voices that filled the room with joyous commotion. They joined hands in a happy dance, singing the *pasuk* in *Tehillim* as they leapt around the room: "For You saved us from our foes and You put our enemies to shame."[5]

The tune was both catchy and moving, and the boys repeated the words over and over, getting swept up in it. Elkanah entered the middle of the circle, dancing with his eyes shut tight in concentration and lips humming the next *pasuk*: "We praised Hashem all day long." The children replied in turn, "And we will forever thank Your Name." They went on like that for a long time, until their legs couldn't carry them any longer and they collapsed, exhausted but laughing with joy, onto the benches scattered across the room.

"Rebbi, maybe we should make a *seudas hoda'ah*? We still haven't celebrated properly and we haven't thanked Hashem enough for miraculously saving us from the Greeks. For six months we learned Torah in secret and we weren't caught!" Naftali wiped his sweaty brow and fanned his face with his hand.

"We should hold the *seudah* in our cave!" cried Yedidya excitedly. "Hey, Reuven, you're too serious. What are you thinking about now?"

---

5. *Tehillim* 44:8–9.

Elkanah entered the middle of the circle,
dancing with his eyes shut tight in concentration.

"I wonder if any of our belongings are still in the cave," Reuven replied, thinking wistfully of the miniature of the Beis HaMikdash he had left there.

"They're probably still there," declared Mahalalel confidently. "Do you think the Greeks actually want our rags?"

"And what about the miniature?" Yehudah asked out loud, voicing Reuven's thoughts. Reuven didn't want to set himself up for disappointment, but Yehudah seemed to have no qualms. "I really hope it's there!" he said optimistically, and broke out in song again, the rest of the boys clapping their hands to the rhythm.

*   *   *

The first session of the special *Beis Din* lasted half an hour. At the end of the meeting, they summarized their conclusions in writing:

B'ezras Hashem Yisbarach

The chief items on our agenda are as follows:

1. Removal of *avodah zarah*, first and foremost from the area of the *Azarah* and Har HaBayis, and then from all of Yerushalayim.
2. Purification of the Kohanim with the ashes of the *parah adumah*, since most of them became *temei meis* during the battles.
3. Weaving and sewing of the *bigdei kehunah*.
4. Manufacture of new *klei shareis*.
5. Repair of the thirteen breaches that the Greeks made in the *Soreg*.
6. Regarding the *Mizbeach* in the *Azarah*, deliberations will resume in another two hours, with the participation of additional *dayanim*.

With remarkable timing, Elkanah was discussing the very same topic with his students.

"Soon, with Hashem's help, the *avodah* of the *korbanos* will resume. What do you think, boys? Can we use the same *Mizbeach* we've always used, or do we need to build a new one?"

The question opened up a fascinating discussion in which the boys took different sides.

"Of course we need a new *Mizbeach*! How can we bring *korbanos* to Hashem on a *Mizbeach* that was used to sacrifice pigs?" Zevulun could hardly bring himself to say such a thing.

"Those horrible Greeks designated the *Mizbeach* for idol worship. We have to destroy it and rebuild it," Yossi agreed with Zevulun.

"A person cannot make something forbidden if it is not his,"[6] said Yehudah, who was of a different opinion. "The *Mizbeach* does not belong to the Greeks, and even if they wanted to they could not designate it for *avodah zarah*."

"So what, but they still sacrificed pigs on it!" hollered Zevulun, his face beet red. "And you want us to bring *korbanos* on it?"

"Boys, please," Elkanah reminded them, "there's nothing personal in this discussion, and we have to respect each other's opinions, even if we don't agree with them."

"There is an *issur* in the Torah to destroy a *Mizbeach*." Naftali, with his extensive knowledge, came to Yehudah's aid. "It says about *avodah zarah*, 'You shall break apart their altars,' and right after that it says, 'You shall not do so to Hashem, your God.'[7] The *Chachamim* learn from here that we are not allowed to break a stone from the *Mizbeach*."[8]

"But they sacrificed pig meat on the *Mizbeach*," Zevulun said, almost in tears.

---

6. *Zevachim* 114a.
7. *Devarim* 12:3–4.
8. Rashi, ibid.

"If it's forbidden to break it, then it's forbidden! You can't do something that's forbidden just because of the way you feel! Your emotions can't override halachah!" yelled Yehudah.

Elkanah raised his hand for quiet. Yehudah's face was wet with perspiration, and Zevulun stood up to get a drink of water, trying to calm down.

"Look, boys. This really is a complicated question. On the one hand, we're dealing with an explicit prohibition in the Torah. On the other hand, our hearts simply will not allow us to offer *korbanos* to Hashem on the *Mizbeach* that was contaminated by the Greeks. When we go up to Yerushalayim, we'll hear what the *Chachamim* ruled on this matter."

The hint that Elkanah dropped with the words, "when we go up to Yerushalayim," was met with cheering. How wonderful! Soon they would be going to Yerushalayim!

*   *   *

At those very same moments, the *dayanim* were grappling with difficult questions on the topic.

A *pasuk* from *Sefer Yechezkel* was what finally led to a decision. The *pasuk*, which discusses the destruction of the First Beis HaMikdash, says, "*U'va'u vah paritzim v'chileluhah* — and wild men will enter it and **profane it**."[9] This means that the moment idolaters entered the *Heichal*, the holy vessels became *chullin*, profane, and they became the property of the Gentiles. If they belong to the Gentiles, then as soon as they are used for *avodah zarah* they become forbidden. The *dayanim* learned from this that since the Greeks entered the Beis HaMikdash, the *Mizbeach* became *chullin*, and once it was used to sacrifice to idols its stones were forbidden.[10]

Most of the judges agreed with this reasoning, and the majority ruled that a new *Mizbeach* must be built.

---

9. *Yechezkel* 7:22.
10. Rashi, *Avodah Zarah* 52b, s.v. *dichsiv u'va'u*.

There was a lot of work to be done. In order to build a new *Mizbeach*, they first had to break apart the old one and then bring whole stones that were untouched by iron, because those were the only kind of stones that may be used for a *Mizbeach*.[11] The project would take at least a week, but there was no choice.

"Maybe we should use the old stones and build a new *Mizbeach* from them," someone suggested to the *dayanim* in a sincere attempt to shorten construction time. "We'll take apart the old *Mizbeach*, and ask a Gentile to break the stones. That will remove their *avodah zarah* status, and we can use them to build a new *Mizbeach*.[12] That'll save precious time!"

"It may sound like a good idea, but for the *Mizbeach* we need whole stones. Even a small crack invalidates a stone,"[13] someone else reminded him.

"So after we take the *Mizbeach* apart, we'll saw the stones down and smooth over any cracks or breaks,"[14] suggested the first Jew boldly. Familiar with the teaching that "a bashful person cannot learn,"[15] he was not ashamed to offer his opinion.

"What will we saw it with? The Torah forbids us from using iron on the stones of the *Mizbeach*!"[16]

The Kohen who was waiting there received clear instructions: Prepare wooden wagons to travel to the Beis Kerem valley and bring back stones suitable for building the *Mizbeach*.[17]

---

11. *Devarim* 27:6.
12. *Avodah Zarah* 52b.
13. *Chullin* 18a.
14. *Avodah Zarah* 52b.
15. Mishnah *Avos* 2:5.
16. *Devarim* 27:5.
17. Mishnah *Middos* 3:4.

Chapter Fifteen

The Ancient Flute

25 KISLEV, IN THE AFTERNOON.

There was a lot of hustle and bustle surrounding the tall house near Har HaBayis(1). Inside the spacious house, whose generous owners had allowed the Chashmonaim to use it as long as they needed to, sat the members of *Beis Din*, ruling on the halachic questions that constantly arose.

The Jews who filled the courtyard stood ready and waiting, joyously fulfilling the special mission that had been entrusted to them. They all had their sights focused on one sublime goal: to reinstate the *avodah* in the Beis HaMikdash.

*　　　　*　　　　*

"Honored *rabbanim*, we are now ready. We are waiting at the gates of the Beis HaMikdash, prepared to clean it. Our hands are eager to rid the *Heichal* of all impurities. Our legs are trembling with the enormity of this task….But most of us are *tamei*. They sent me to ask who is allowed to enter, and where?" The gray-bearded Jew with the piercing dark eyes gazed in respect at the members of *Beis Din* and awaited their instructions.

The answer came immediately. "Only Kohanim, preferably Kohanim who are *tahor*, may enter the *Heichal*(11). If there are no Kohanim who are *tahor*, even those who are *tamei* may enter, and they should remove the idols from the *Heichal*,"[1] instructed an

---

1. Rambam, *Hilchos Beis HaBechirah* 7:23.

elder Kohen in a sharp voice. "The area of the *Azarah* may be cleansed by Leviyim and Yisraelim."

The Jew turned to go, a bounce in his step. "How wonderful that the Sages can answer our halachic questions out in the open, and we can follow their directives without fear!" he thought to himself, savoring the moment.

In this ruling, the Sages based themselves on a *pasuk* which discusses the purification of the First Beis HaMikdash from the idols placed there by King Achaz. His son Chizkiyahu, who ruled after him, set out to cleanse the Beis HaMikdash and the *pasuk* describes how he did so:

"The Kohanim came within the House of Hashem to purify it, and they removed all the impurity that they found in the *Heichal* of Hashem to the courtyard of the House of Hashem, and the Leviyim received it to take it out to the Kidron Valley outside."[2]

The hundreds of people in the entrance to the Beis HaMikdash listened intently to the answer, which was delivered in a booming voice by the gray-bearded Jew. There were no pure Kohanim present; they were all *temei meis* because they had come into contact with corpses during battle. With no other choice, the impure Kohanim entered the *Heichal*, shaking in fear and awe of the holy place. They removed every shred of impurity from the *Kodesh HaKodashim*(12) and from the *Heichal*(11). Idols, large and small, were taken out to the *Azarah*, and from there they were carried away in disgust, far from Har HaBayis(1).

A Jew in stained work clothes entered the *Beis Din* with heavy steps. "I have been put in charge of dismantling the *Mizbeach*(7) in the *Azarah*," he said. "What are we supposed to do with the stones?"

He sat down in a chair and closed his eyes in exhaustion while the *dayanim* debated the question.

---

2. *II Divrei HaYamim* 29:16.

"Dear Jew!" The call jolted him from his brief slumber. He stood up at once and leaned over to hear the *dayan's* next words. "We have decided that even though the stones are technically *chullin* and may be used for other purposes, it would not be proper *kavod* for the *Mizbeach* if we reuse them. Therefore, you should store them away."[3]

"Where?" he asked.

"It would be best to store them somewhere in the Beis HaMikdash," replied the *av beis din.* "Where exactly? That will be decided by the Kohanim in charge."

*   *   *

Off in the distance, they could hear the voice of the crier growing louder:

"Anyone who has wool strings of *techeiles, argaman,* or *tola'as shani,* is asked to bring them to Kiponus Gate urgently! Anyone who has wool strings of *techeiles, argaman,* or *tola'as shani,* is asked to bring them to Kiponus Gate urgently!"

Silence reigned in the two-floor house next to Kiponus Gates(28), a silence uncharacteristic of the dozens of women who sat there.[4] The women were busy weaving *bigdei kehunah.* They had plenty of linen thread, but the war had produced a shortage of colored wool. The crier made his way around the city, and slowly the necessary wool began to arrive, whether in whole bundles or single strands.

Before the Greeks entered the Mikdash, the Chamber of Pinchas, Keeper of the Priestly Garments(52), was used to store the *bigdei kehunah.*[5] Each Kohen needed four garments: a *kesones* (shirt), *avneit* (belt), *michnasayim* (trousers), and *mitznefes* (turban). Each *mishmeres* had its own clothes, reserved just for them, so there were enough

---

3. *Avodah Zarah* 52b.

4. *Kiddushin* 49b.

5. Mishnah *Middos* 1:4; Mishnah *Tamid* 5:3.

Temple Mount

West

South

North

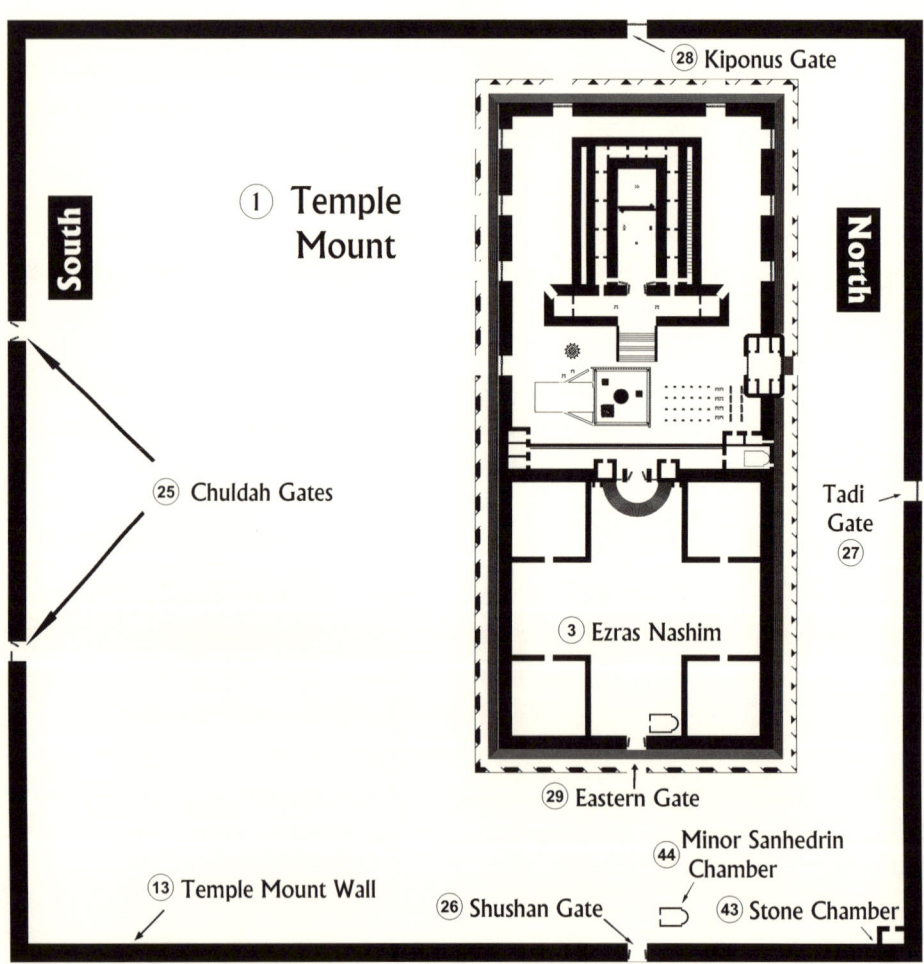

(28) Kiponus Gate

(1) Temple Mount

(25) Chuldah Gates

Tadi Gate (27)

(3) Ezras Nashim

(29) Eastern Gate

Minor Sanhedrin (44) Chamber

(13) Temple Mount Wall

(26) Shushan Gate

(43) Stone Chamber

East

sets of clothes there for tens of thousands of Kohanim! The Greeks plundered those as well, and righteous Jewish women volunteered their services to renew the supply of *bigdei kehunah.*

"Ladies, work quickly!" the woman in charge, wife of a Kohen, urged them. "The inauguration of Beis HaMikdash will take place in about a week, and we need a few hundred sets of clothing ready by then."

A short woman strode into the room and triumphantly pulled an enormous ball of *techeiles* out of her basket. "My daughter-in-law is such a *tzaddeikes*!" she told the woman who gratefully collected the treasure from her. "That string was supposed to be used to make her a new Shabbos dress. But she, righteous woman that she is, gave it to the Mikdash instead. 'The *bigdei kehunah* are more important,' she told me."

The other women nodded in admiration.

"Oh, that reminds me!" cried a woman sitting nearby. "My Shabbos headscarf! It's woven from *argaman* threads! I'll ask the *Chachamim* if I can unravel it and use it for *bigdei kehunah.*"

*   *   *

A Jew who was actually quite young, but looked much older than his age, entered the *Beis Din*. His face was flushed with excitement, and the *dayanim* waited patiently to find out why .

"I was able to save cymbals and a flute that were used in the First Beis HaMikdash!" he said in elation. Then he told his heart-stopping story to a mesmerized audience. "I am a Levi. When the Greeks invaded the Beis HaMikdash, I was in one of the *Leshachos Klei HaShir*(50), the Musical Instruments Chambers. I was busy cleaning the harps at the time. I heard noise from outside, but I paid no attention to it. Suddenly, someone, I don't remember who, ran into the chamber in shock. 'Run!' he shouted. 'The Greeks are here! Our lives are in danger!'

"I was paralyzed, frozen in place. How could I let the holy instruments fall into unclean hands? What do I do? The other man sighed and placed a hand over his eyes. I could tell that he had just seen terrible things, things he would never forget. I began to think feverishly, and in a split second a few different ideas flashed through my mind, each one less practical than the one before. Then I remembered the ancient flute from the time of Moshe Rabbeinu, and the cymbals that were played in the First Beis HaMikdash.[6] 'These I have to save,' I thought to myself."

The man was so engrossed in his tale that he didn't notice how more and more people quietly slipped into the room, listening with bated breath to his incredible story.

"I ran to the special compartment we're they're kept, grabbed them, and then wondered where to go next. How would I get out of the Beis HaMikdash? From the entrance of the *Lishkas Klei HaShir*, I could hear sounds of battle. I turned on my heels and went through the tunnel[7] that connects that chamber to *Sha'ar HaShir*, also known as *Sha'ar Beis HaMoked*(32), Pyre Hall Gate.[8] Carefully, I peered out of the opening of the *Beis HaMoked* in the direction of the *Cheil*(2),[9] and my face fell. I saw the Greeks standing next to the *Soreg*(14), breaking the lattice fence with heavy hammers."[10]

"It was obvious that the Greeks would attack the *Soreg*(14),"[11] interrupted the *av beis din*. "Up until that point, they were prohibited from crossing the *Soreg* and entering the *Cheil*,[12] so they took their revenge on it."

After a few seconds, the Levi continued. "I almost gave up,

---

6. *Arachin* 10b.
7. Mishnah *Middos* 2:6, *Tiferes Yisrael* #79.
8. Ibid., #78.
9. Mishnah *Middos* 1:7.
10. Ibid., 2:3.
11. *Tosfos Yom Tov*, ibid.
12. Mishnah *Keilim* 1:8.

The Azarah

West

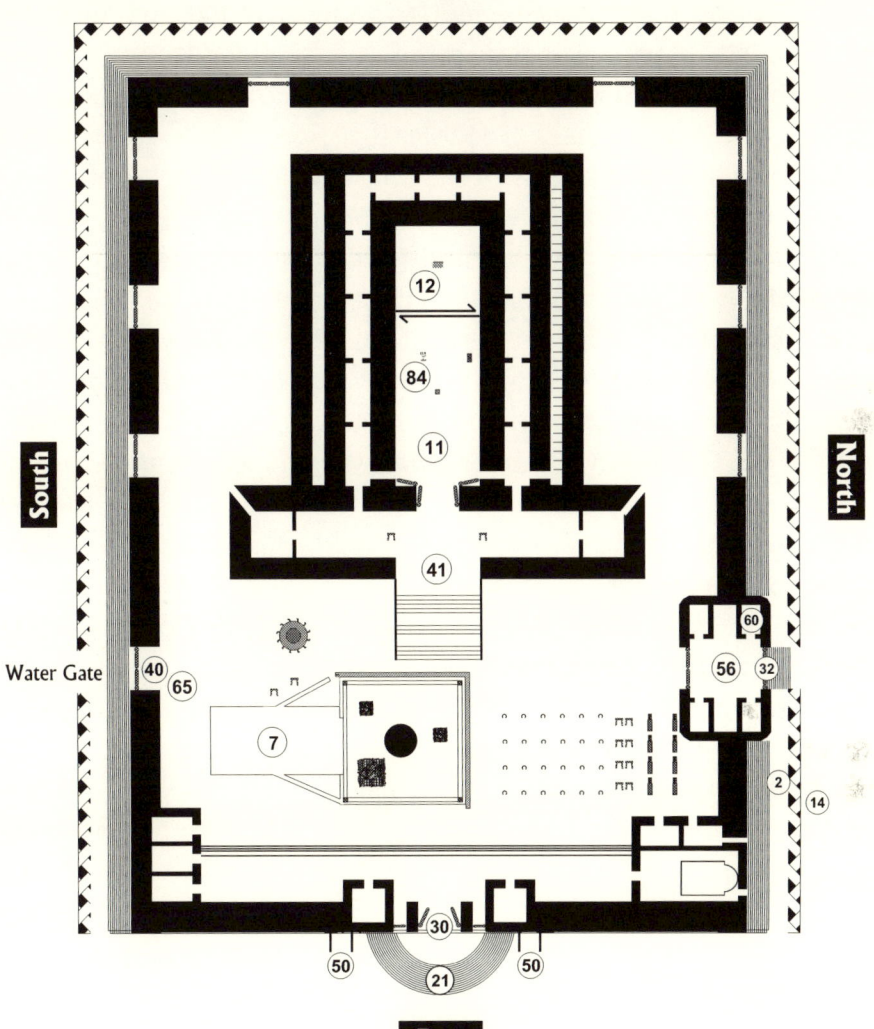

South

North

Water Gate

East

2. *Cheil*	32. Pyre Hall Gate (Music Gate)
7. *Mizbeach* (Altar)	40. Water Gate
11. *Heichal*	41. Entrance to *Ulam*
12. *Kodesh HaKodashim*	50. Musical Instruments Chambers
14. *Soreg* (lattice fence)	56. The Pyre Hall
21. 15 Steps ascending from *Ezras Nashim* to *Ezras Yisrael*	60. Small Pyre Chamber
	65. Avtinas Family Chamber
30. Nikanor Gate	84. Menorah

but then I had an idea: the *Beis HaMoked HaKatan*(60), the Small
Pyre Chamber![13] I slipped inside and raced down the steps that
lead to the *Beis HaMoked HaKatan*, tripping over my own feet. I fell
over and the instruments flew out of my hand. With superhuman
strength, I picked myself up, grabbed the holy instruments, and
kept on running."

His voice dropped and took on a pained tone. "Only after-
wards did I notice that the cymbals were damaged with a dent."[14]

"You did a great deed by saving the instruments," the *av beis
din* comforted him with his reassuring words. "I think that out of
all the thousands of instruments, these are the only two that remain! Don't worry. It's better that we have slightly damaged, holy
cymbals, than undamaged cymbals gathering dust in the basement of the Greek king! I'm sure that we can have them repaired."

"What happened after you ran down the steps of the *Beis
HaMoked HaKatan*?" the listeners were in suspense and they
wanted to know the end of the story.

The Levi wiped his sweaty brow and continued. "As I ran, I
thought I might find some sort of tunnel I could escape through.
I reached the mikveh, but there was no tunnel there.[15] I sat down
for a minute to figure out what to do next, and I decided to hide
the flute and the cymbals inside a deep hole in the wall. Maybe
one day I'd be able to come back for them. But there was something else; a thought that pecked at my brain and wouldn't leave
me alone. If I died soon *al kiddush HaShem*, I wanted to die pure.
So I quickly immersed in the mikveh that was there,[16] and turned
around to go.

---

13. Mishnah *Middos* 1:6.
14. *Arachin* 10b.
15. *Bartenura* and *Tiferes Yisrael*, Mishnah *Middos* 1:9.
16. Mishnah *Tamid* 1:1.

"I sat down for a minute to figure out what to do next."

"I went back up the steps to Pyre Hall, *Beis HaMoked*(56), and stopped there, at a loss. What should I do now? If I went out to the *Cheil*(2), I would be caught by the Greeks. I peeked out of the doorway that goes from the *Beis HaMoked* to the *Azarah*;[17] maybe I would able to sneak out somehow. But to my misfortune, a Greek soldier was looking right in my direction and he saw me right away. He ran over to me, grabbed me with an iron fist and dragged me to a spot across from the Entrance to the *Ulam*(41) where the Greeks had gathered all the Jews they'd found inside the Beis HaMikdash. I thought that perhaps they were about to murder us and I was glad that I had immersed in the mikveh.

"We stood there in petrified silence for many long minutes. A number of Greek soldiers were guarding us to make sure we wouldn't escape, and we stood and waited. For what, we didn't know.

"Our eyes were fixed on Nikanor Gate(30), through which a Greek nobleman arrogantly walked, accompanied by his wife — a Jewess! Miriam, the daughter of Bilgah HaKohen.[18] This traitorous woman walked over to the *Mizbeach*(7), kicked it with her shoe and shouted, "*Lukus, Lukus*! Wolf, Wolf! How much longer will you consume Yisrael's money without even protecting them in difficult times?"

A disapproving hiss filled the room. How low could a Jewish girl fall? To shout at the *Mizbeach* and call it a wolf that consumes the meat of the *korbanos* but does not protect the Jews from danger and misfortune?!

His listeners responded with pained groans, and when it was quiet again he continued. "After waiting for a while, we realized that the Greeks were simply scared to enter the *Heichal*(11). They

---

17. Mishnah *Middos* 1:7.
18. *Sukkah* 56b.

knew how holy it was and they feared for their lives. The commander sat on his horse and did nothing except announce time and again, 'Who wants to go in first?'

"Silence. The soldiers weren't willing to risk their lives.

"The second-in-command whispered something in his ear and the commander's eyes lit up.

"'Listen up, Greeks and Jews! Whoever goes in first can choose one of the precious gold vessels of the Mikdash for himself.

"This guarantee did nothing to assuage the Greeks' fear, but to everyone's shock, a Hellenistic Jew stepped forward. His name was Yosef Meshisa, and he brazenly declared, 'I will enter!'

Boos and jeers rose up from the ranks of the Jews. What a bootlicker! Paving the way for the Greeks to enter the Beis HaMikdash! They would see him go in and come out unharmed, and they would no longer be afraid to enter.

Yosef Meshisa went in with broad, confident strides, clicking his hobnailed shoes on the holy floor. A few minutes later, we could hear the sound of a heavy object being dragged around. The *misyavein* appeared in the doorway, hauling the golden Menorah(84) with considerable difficulty! Ah! The holy Menorah! It was the first and probably the last time I would see it. Two of its lamps were still burning, their flames reflected in the radiant gold.

"This was too much, even for the Greeks. 'An ordinary citizen cannot use such a magnificent vessel!' barked the commander, who 'forgot' the promise he had made two minutes earlier. 'Go back in and take a different vessel. The Menorah will be sent to the King!'[19]

"At that point, I realized that no one was watching us. The soldiers were engrossed in the drama that was unfolding and they weren't looking at us at all. Very quietly, I tiptoed backwards.

---

19. *Bereishis Rabbah* 65.

When I reached the entrance I broke out into a run, and I ran and ran until I reached safety.

"This morning, when the Beis HaMikdash returned to our hands, I wanted to go in immediately to make sure the instruments were still there, but since I was *temei meis* I was forbidden by the decree of the Sages to cross the *Soreg*(14).[20] I looked for a Yisraeli who was *tahor*, and when I found one I gave him exact instructions where to find the holy instruments I had hidden. He went and just reported back to me — they are still there!" There was a glimmer of satisfaction in the Levi's eyes.

The words "a Yisraeli who was *tahor*" galvanized the *dayanim*. "We're desperately looking for Jews who are pure, even Yisraelim! Can you ask that man to come here?"

Without another word, the Levi disappeared, on his way to fulfill the Sages' request.

---

20. Mishnah *Keilim* 1:8.

Chapter Sixteen

Discovery in the Oil Chamber

A small, unified group could be seen crossing Har HaBayis. The group made its way cautiously up the steps over the Water Gate(40) and was swallowed up in the Avtinas Family Chamber, *Lishkas Beis Avtinas*(65).[1] The members of the Avtinas family, responsible for preparing the *ketores*,[2] had come to check out the situation in their chamber.

Although they were not surprised by the sight that met their eyes, it pained them terribly nonetheless. The chamber was emptied of its vessels and incense, which had apparently been ransacked by the enemy. The items they found in the chamber indicated that the Greeks had used this room as an office. There was a stone idol on the table and one of the young men in the group grabbed it in disgust and broke it on the floor.

The head of the family tried to come terms with reality. "We have to make new *keilim* and new *ketores*," he said, gently putting down the three vessels he had brought with him. These were the only vessels he had managed to smuggle out before the Greeks arrived. There was a mortar from the days of Moshe Rabbeinu,[3] as well as a golden *kaf* and *machtah*, the spoon and firepan that the

---

1. Mishnah *Middos* 1:1.
2. *Yoma* 38a.
3. *Arachin* 10b.

Kohen Gadol used to offer the *ketores* in the *Kodesh HaKodashim*(12) on Yom Kippur.

"This is a problem," said the elderly *dayan* after the Avtinases told the temporary *Beis Din* that they would need to make new *keilim* and *ketores*. "How much time do you need to prepare new *ketores*?"

"At least two weeks," replied the head of the family. "We have to purify ourselves first," he added apologetically.

"Of course. Some of the ingredients in the *ketores* are foods, which are *mekabel tum'ah*."

"Correct. That's why we've always made sure to prepare it when we're *tahor*. It will take a week for us to become *tahor* from *tum'as meis*, and it shouldn't take longer than a week to make the *ketores* itself, assuming we can obtain all the ingredients easily."

The *dayan* frowned. "Two weeks is a long time. Make it as quick as you can. We hope to begin bringing *korbanos* within a week."

"Well, in any case, at the moment we have enough *ketores* for a few days," the head of the Avtinas family said, to the absolute delight of the *dayanim*. "One of our elders sneaked out ten *manim* of *ketores*, a ten-day supply.[4] We also managed to save the *ma'aleh ashan*, the ingredient that makes the smoke from the *ketores* rise straight up. We were worried that the Greeks would use it to offer incense to idols, *chas v'chalilah*."[5]

"You did well. Now go on, and may Hashem bless you with success!"

They left the *Beis Din* and sat down to organize their search for the rare ingredients that make up the *ketores*. Soon after they left, one of the family members was back with a question.

"How much *ketores* should we make? Enough for a year, or six months' worth?"

---

4. *Kerisos* 6a.
5. *Yoma* 38a.

"Just make a three-month supply,"[6] answered the *dayanim*. "On Rosh Chodesh Nissan you'll purchase new ingredients with the money from the *machatzis ha-shekel* collection in the month of Adar."[7]

*   *   *

Two men stood on the wall of the *Azarah*. One of the elder Kohanim, a leader of the revolt, stood next to a relatively young *dayan* and together they looked out at the *Azarah*.

The area of the *Azarah* was humming with activity. Men ran to and fro on the marble floor, carrying more and more idols out.

The *dayan* spread his hands wide in gratitude. "*'Hodu laShem ki tov, ki l'olam chasdo!'*[8] I feel so blessed to witness with my own eyes the purification of the Beis HaMikdash! Very soon we'll be able to bring *korbanos* again. Just the thought of it makes my heart sing!"

"It wasn't an easy decision," said the Kohen. A cool breeze whipped across his shoulders and he shivered. "We deliberated back and forth whether or not it was appropriate to rebel openly against the Greeks and endanger the few remaining religious Jews. Perhaps it was better to continue keeping the mitzvos in secret and live with the terrible decrees until Hashem had mercy on us? In the end, it was Matisyahu ben Yochanan who made the decision, and we went out to fight."

"It all sounds so simple," said the *dayan*, "but I'm sure in reality you went out to fight with hearts pounding."

"We did, but we had so many open miracles. And look, *baruch Hashem* we're purifying the Beis HaMikdash now!"

The two lapsed into silence for a moment, and then the Kohen spoke up again. "The danger is not over yet, though. Now we're here and the Greeks are gone, but I suspect they won't give up

---

6. *Kerisos* 6b.

7. Mishnah *Shekalim* 4:5.

8. *Tehillim* 107:1.

control of this Land so fast. The forces of *tum'ah* won't allow the pleasing scent of the *korbanos* to ascend so easily. I'm sure the Greeks will try to recapture Yerushalayim. If they succeed, their revenge will be cruel, indeed."

The elderly Kohen gazed off in the distance at the mountains surrounding them. Green slopes were splayed out below, their bright color a sight for sore eyes. The skies above them were a deep shade of gray and the scent of rain hung in the air.

The Kohen gave a sudden jolt. "What am I worrying about?" he berated himself. "The One Who has helped up until now will continue to help us!"

The *dayan* approached the corner of the wall, trying to get a better view of the work on the *Mizbeach*. "Look, they're already taking apart the *Sovev*," he told the Kohen, filling him on the background to the *Beis Din*'s decision. "It was a complicated question. Personally, I was against destroying the *Mizbeach*, because of the explicit prohibition in the Torah, 'You shall not do so to Hashem, your God.'[9] But the majority voted in favor, and we follow the majority.[10] We have to accept their opinion."

*   *   *

The fifteen workers and their supervisor stopped at the entrance to the Oil Chamber(49) in horror. Havoc and destruction were everywhere. Broken bottles of wine, smashed oil jugs and shards of pottery were scattered on the floor, swimming in pools of wine and oil. It was clear that the Greeks had tried their hardest not to leave a single vessel whole. The supervisor grasped his head in his hands in shock. "This chamber is big,[11] almost like a small hall. There were hundreds of bottles of wine for *nesachim*

---

9. *Devarim* 12:4.
10. *Shemos* 23:2.
11. Mishnah *Middos* 2:5.

Ezras Nashim

West

South

North

East

Nikanor Gate
(30)

15
Steps
(21)

Oil
Chamber
(49)

(50) Musical Instruments
Chambers

Metzora'im's
Chamber
(48)

(3) Ezras Nashim

(15) → Wall of
Azarah

Nazarite's
Chamber
(46)

Minor
Sanhedrin
Chamber
(45)

Wood
Chamber
(47)

(29) Eastern Gate
↓

(20) 12 Steps ascending
from Cheil to Azarah

(2) Cheil

(14) Soreg
(lattice fence)

and so many jugs of oil for *menachos,* and look what's left of it!" He entered carefully, trying not to slip. "Oh no! They were here, too! The oil for the Menorah…"

"The oil for the Menorah was kept separate from the oil for the *menachos?*" asked one of the workers, puzzled. "Why? Aren't they both made from olives?"

"A number of different kinds of oil are produced from olives," explained the supervisor patiently, moving aside a huge broken jug that blocked his way. "For *menachos,* any type of olive oil can be used, but for the Menorah you need special olive oil known as 'kasis.' That's the first, best-quality oil that comes out of the olives the first time they're pressed, before they're ground."[12]

"Villains!" spat another worker as he carefully collected some of the bigger shards. "It looks like they came in here just to defile the oil.[13] They didn't even use it for anything. It was destruction for destruction's sake."

"It's not hard to understand why." One of workers, a wise man, got up from the floor. "Oil hints to wisdom, the wisdom of Torah.[14] The Greeks wanted to destroy the Torah along with everything that represents it, so they systematically defiled the oil and poured it all out."[15]

*   *   *

The supervisor clapped his hands. "Okay, enough talking. Let's divide up the work among ourselves. Every pair of workers will clean a different area of the chamber."

The area of the oil for the Menorah was assigned to Elchanan

---

12. *Menachos* 86a.

13. *Imrei Emes — Likutim, Shabbos* 21b.

14. *Menachos* 85b.

15. *Bnei Yissaschar,* Kislev 7.

and Gamliel. They hauled over a large wooden crate and started to toss oily, broken fragments of jugs inside. Elchanan leaned over to pick up an especially big piece of pottery from the corner of the room. He was about to throw it into the crate when he noticed a wide crack between the wall and the floor.

"Gamliel?" His voice took on a strange tone and his friend came right away. "I think there's something there. Give me a candle, please."

Gamliel, always equipped with whatever was needed, lit a candle and passed it to Elchanan, who held it next to the crack.

"Hey, there's a sealed jug there!" At Elchanan's exuberant cry, the workers hurried over from all corners of the chamber.

"Don't touch it," said Gamliel with a touch of urgency in his voice. "We're *tamei*!"

"You're right. I won't touch it, but let's see whose seal it is."

The workers excitedly moved away the shards that blocked the crack and tried to widen it a bit. Elchanan stooped over again and tilted the candle into the space. On the oily, orange jug, they could clearly make out four letters: הן גד. There were other letters, too, but they were too blurred to be legible.

No one dared voice it out loud, but all of them shared the same hope: could this be pure oil?

"An earthenware utensil does not become *tamei* if you touch the outside of it,"[16] claimed one worker, leaning on his shovel. "We can touch it even if we're *tamei*."

"There are some *temei'im* who defile a vessel by carrying it,"[17] the knowledgeable worker argued back. "None of us has been careful about the laws of *tum'ah* and *taharah* during the last few months. Don't touch that jug!"

---

16. *Chullin* 24b.

17. *Tosfos, Shabbos* 21a, s.v. *she'hayah*.

A few of the workers, who had already bent down to pick it up, recoiled at once.

"Gamliel," the supervisor instructed, "go to the *Beis Din*'s temporary location, and ask them to send us someone *tahor*. The rest of you," he turned to the others, "carry on with your work."

The Jew who had confirmed that the flute and cymbals were still in their hiding place in the *Beis HaMoked* now had another mission to carry out. He was to rescue the unidentified jug from the crevice in the Oil Chamber.

Chapter Seventeen
The Iron Menorah

A few more hammer blows to widen the crack, a few strong yanks, and the small clay jug was released from its hiding place. It was stained with mud, and based on its size the men estimated that it contained three and a half *log* of oil.

On Har HaBayis, the *tahor* Jew who extricated the jug from the crack gingerly wiped it off until the inscription was legible, and this is what it said:[1] שמן כתית למנורה יהוידע כהן גדול.

The jug was carefully taken to *Beis Din*, where it was opened. A great joy spread across the faces of everyone present.

"Hashem is pleased with our hard work!" cried one of the elder Kohanim with a tremor in his voice. "Perhaps this is a sign from Heaven that we should light the Menorah today and not wait until the new *Mizbeach* is inaugurated?"

"Interesting," murmured the Jew who had removed the jug from the crack. "I wonder why the Kohen Gadol put his stamp on the jug. That is highly unusual."

Word of the amazing discovery spread throughout Yerushalayim: A jug of pure oil[2] with the seal of the Kohen Gadol was found in the Oil Chamber(49)![3]

*　　　　*　　　　*

1. *Al HaTeshuos*, p. 215.
2. *Shabbos* 21b.
3. *Gilyon HaShas*, ibid.

The small clay jug was released from its hiding place.

Beis Din requested that all bystanders leave the room so that they could deliberate a number of pressing questions that had arisen in light of the discovery of the pure oil jug. The first and most important question was whether or not it was permitted to light the Menorah even though the *avodah* of the *korbanos* was not back in operation.

"There is no connection between these two *avodos*,"[4] most of the *dayanim* ruled. "We can and should light the Menorah, even though the *Mizbeach* is still under construction."

"And where will we get fire to light the Menorah?" asked one of the *dayanim*. "The fire is always taken from one of the Menorah lights that is still burning,[5] or from the Pyre on the *Mizbeach*.[6] Now we don't have either one!"

In the end, *Beis Din* ruled that the source of the fire was not critical, and the Menorah could be lit from ordinary fire.[7]

"Just a minute!" All heads in the room swiveled to face a distinguished-looking Kohen. "We're busy discussing where to get fire from, but meanwhile we don't even have a Menorah! Yosef Meshisa…"

"Yes, Yosef Meshisha the tzaddik took it out of the *Heichal*," sighed a black-haired Kohen with a salt-and-pepper beard.

"Yosef Meshisa the tzaddik?!" The question reverberated through the room and filled the air with dozens of question marks.

"Yes," said the blacked-bearded *dayan* with another sigh. He stood up in place, a look of pain etched across his face. "This morning we heard only half the story. Later, my son told me the continuation. He heard it from his friend, a Kohen who was there

---

4. *Shevet HaLevi*, Chanukah, p. 105.

5. *Shabbos* 22b.

6. Mishnah *Tamid* 6:1.

7. *Shevet HaLevi*, Chanukah, p. 106.

when it happened." The *dayan* grew quiet, and it was obvious that it was difficult for him to speak.

"Yosef Meshisa the tzaddik," he repeated, tears glistening in his eyes. "After the commander told him to go back inside and take another vessel, he refused. No amount of begging, pleading, promises, or threats could make him change his mind. Yosef would not agree to go back in. He just said over and over, 'Woe to me that I angered my Creator.'[8]

"This Jew sacrificed his life to avoid transgressing Hashem's command, even though a moment earlier he had deliberately transgressed! Do you see what level a Jew can reach? How great is the power of *teshuvah*! And how great is the power of the Beis HaMikdash! Just a brief stay in the *Heichal*(11) caused a complete transformation![9] Yosef became a different person! The commander would not give in. He inflicted Yosef with excruciating forms of torture until his *neshamah* left him."

The Kohen's voiced cracked. He knew Yosef personally; they had been neighbors before he became a *misyavein*. Yosef's heroism and courage deeply affected the *dayan*.

An older *dayan* of average height and flaming eyes broke the silence. "The Menorah that Yosef Meshisa, *zichrono livrachah*, removed from the *Heichal* has disappeared. We have pure oil, but no Menorah to light."

"We'll make a temporary Menorah," suggested the elder sage of the Kohanim in a raspy voice. "It would take a long time to make a gold Menorah, and I'm not sure we could even find the amount of gold we would need.[10] We'll make a temporary Menorah from some other material."

---

8. *Bereishis Rabbah* 65.
9. The Ponovezher Rav, Rav Yosef Shlomo Kahaneman *zt"l*.
10. *Rosh Hashanah* 24b.

The room filled with the buzz of conversation. Some of the *dayanim* held that any type of metal was suitable for the Menorah, but wood, glass and earthenware were not. Others claimed that the Menorah could be made from any material except earthenware.[11]

"I have sheets of iron in my attic," offered a *dayan* hesitantly when the noise died down. "They're made from excellent quality metal, and I have no particular use for them."

His intention was clear: perhaps they could be used to make a new Menorah. "But they might be *tamei* with *tum'as meis*," said the *av beis din* uncertainly.

"They're raw sheets of metal that were not made into or used as vessels, so they cannot become *tamei*."[12]

"Acceptable!" ruled the *dayanim* unanimously.

"Well then, matters are progressing nicely," said the elder sage of the Kohanim. "But who will melt down the iron and cast a Menorah from it, with all the details and nuances it requires?"

"My cousin is a blacksmith." The speaker took a sip from the cup in front of him. "As of yesterday, he was still *tahor*. I hope he hasn't become *tamei* since then. He has hands of gold, and I'm sure he could do the job quickly."

"What about the *gevi'im*, *kaftorim* and *perachim*, the Menorah's decorative goblets, balls and flowers?"[13]

"If the Menorah is not made of gold, none of those things are necessary," ruled *Beis Din*. "The blacksmith should craft a center branch and then solder six branches to it. On top, he should make bowls to hold the oil; each bowl should hold half a *log*."[14]

* * *

---

11. *Menachos* 28b.

12. Rambam, *Hilchos Keilim* 8:1.

13. *Shemos* 25:33.

14. *Menachos* 28a.

An older Jew with broad shoulders, dressed in simple work clothes and with a large yarmulke on his head, arrived. He looked at the *dayanim* with pure, innocent eyes.

"It's a great privilege for me," he began in a deep, humble voice. "That I, Mordechai ben Yaakov, should fashion the Menorah for the Beis HaMikdash!" He didn't waste words, and got right down to business. "Is there another *tahor* Jew who can help me?"

The Yisraeli who had already lent a hand a few times that day was ready and willing to undertake another request from *Beis Din.* "I'd be happy to help make the Menorah," he said simply.

The blacksmith and his newfound assistant left the room but were quickly summoned back inside.

"One moment! There's something else," said a young *dayan.* "Tell me, please, how did you get the oil jug out of the crack where it was hidden?"

"I'm so sorry," interrupted another *dayan* in a tone of respect mixed with impatience. "But I think it might be better for you to speak about this later. Time is of the essence and the Menorah must be ready soon!"

"I'm not merely asking out of curiosity," explained the young *dayan.* "This is something we need to know. I want to make sure that no non-Jew moved the jug from its place. That would have made it *tamei* even if they hadn't opened it."[15]

"Oh, that is a good question! The answer is very important," agreed the *av beis din.* "Tell us how you freed the jug."

"I don't think anyone moved it before I did," the Jew said, twirling the *peyos* behind his right ear. It felt awkward to be in the spotlight. "The jug was wedged deep inside the crevice, and it took a lot of effort to get it out. I tried to do it gently so that the jug wouldn't break, but I'm sure no one else attempted to take it before that."

The *av beis din* nodded his head and stroked his beard. "It could

---

15. *Tosfos, Shabbos* 21b, s.v. *she'hayah.*

be that even if it wasn't underground but just tossed on the ground, it would be permissible to use the oil inside, because any non-Jew who saw a sealed jug wouldn't have left it there without breaking it open to see if it contained valuable gold or diamonds."[16]

The blacksmith and his assistant hurried off to do their work, but in the two-story house that was the *Beis Din*'s temporary dwelling they still had not found answers to all their questions and the *dayanim* had their hands full.

"*Ribbono shel Olam*," the elder Kohen sighed. He lifted his eyes, which glowed with faith and a passionate love for Hashem. "We did our part. From this point on, all we can do is hope for Your mercy. You can surely send us a Kohen who is *tahor* to light the Menorah."

"Maybe one of the *tahor* Yisraelim can light the Menorah," suggested a young Kohen who was moved by the elder Kohen's deep pain and pure hope.

"A Yisraeli?!" was everyone's astonished reply.

"Yes. As far as we know, there is not a single Kohen in the entire area who is *tahor*. Where does it say in the Torah that a non-Kohen may not light the Menorah?" the younger man reiterated his position.

There was silence in the room. Indeed, there was no such prohibition in the Torah. Nevertheless, the idea didn't sit well with them.

"It seems you are correct, and the lighting may be performed by a non-Kohen as well,"[17] said the *av beis din* slowly. "But entry to the *Heichal* is permitted only for Kohanim.[18] If a non-Kohen cannot enter the *Heichal*, how can he light the Menorah?"

"Maybe he could use a long rod?" suggested someone in the corner.

---

16. Ran, ibid.
17. Rambam, *Hilchos Bi'as HaMikdash* 9:7.
18. Rambam, *Hilchos Beis HaBechirah* 7:19–21.

"It would be complicated to maneuver a pole that is fifty *amos* long and use it to light the lights of the Menorah!"

"What if we put the Menorah in the *Azarah* and have the Yisraeli light it there?"[19]

"I think it's better to have a Kohen who is *tamei* light it in the *Heichal* than to have a non-Kohen light it in the *Azarah*. *Tum'ah hutrah b'tzibbur* — when a majority of the public is *tamei*, it is permitted."[20]

"*Tum'ah* is permitted *b'tzibbur* only when the *avodah* in the Beis HaMikdash is being performed as usual.[21] We'll wait another week until the Kohanim become purified."

There were many different opinions and the question continued to hang in the balance.

"*Rabbosai!*" cried the spirited *dayan* who was serving as the temporary clerk. He banged on the table hard. "It's time for *Minchah*. Let's ask Hashem to grant us the wisdom and understanding to reach the correct decision."

"There's one more thing that's not entirely clear to us," someone spoke up. The men, who were already busy tying their sashes in preparation for *tefillah*,[22] stopped and looked up. "The oil that was found is only enough for one day. What we will we do tomorrow? And the next day? And the next? We need more pure olive oil urgently!"

The *av beis din*'s answer was short and to the point. "One option is to produce new oil in Yerushalayim on the day we become

---

19. Rambam, *Hilchos Bi'as HaMikdash* 9:7. See *Chasam Sofer, Derashos l'Chanukah*, vol. 1, p. 67, who explains that in fact that is what they did, and that is why it says in *Al HaNissim*, "*v'hidliku neiros **b'chatzros kadshecha*** — and they lit lamps **in the courtyards of Your Sanctuary**." Thus the miracle was publicized, because it was visible to all.

20. *Pesachim* 77a.

21. *Sefas Emes.*

22. *Shabbos* 10a.

tahor, in another week.[23] The other option is to send a messenger up north, to the portion of the tribe of Asher. There we will almost certainly find pure oil. It's a four-day journey each way,[24] so it will take at least a week for the messenger to go back and forth."

"Azriel!" he instructed the messenger of *Beis Din*. "We are going to operate on both fronts. You'll head up north today, and at the same time, in another week, we'll press olives for oil here in Yerushalayim." He turned around and the *chazan* started *Minchah*.

The *tefillah* was recited with an outpouring of emotion and exceptional closeness to Hashem. The events of the past day were still fresh in everyone's minds, and they had so much to be grateful for! They had witnessed the hand of Hashem accompanying them every step of the way. With His help, they had captured Yerushalayim from the enemy, opened up the *batei midrash*, and brought back the sound of Torah learning. Hundreds were working hard to cleanse and purify the Beis HaMikdash, and the new *Mizbeach* would be ready soon.

"How can we repay Hashem for all His kindness? We will never finish praising Him! *Ribbono shel Olam*," the *dayanim* prayed from the depths of their hearts, "bring us a Kohen who is *tahor* to light the Menorah for us!"

*   *   *

A little while later, the voice of the crier once again echoed through the streets of the newly restored city:

"Kohanim who are *tahor* are requested to appear in the Beis HaMikdash urgently! Kohanim who are *tahor* are requested to appear in the Beis HaMikdash urgently!"

---

23. *Beis Yosef, Orach Chaim* 670.

24. Ran, *Shabbos* 21b.

Chapter Eighteen

Bright Idea

The battle cries that rose up in the distance caught Isamar the Kohen in the middle of skinning the slaughtered bull that hung from the *Nanasin*(79), the low pillars used for flaying animals.[1] Isamar was blessed with sharp ears and was the first to hear the sound and understand what it meant — the Greeks were coming!

He paled. At once, he abandoned his work on the bull and ran over to the entrance of the *Lishkas HaGazis*(53), sprinted across it, escaped from the entrance facing the *Cheil*(2),[2] and from there raced over to Tadi Gate(27). With his heart pounding furiously and his lips dry, he ran through the alleyways of Yerushalayim, narrowly missing numerous encounters with one battalion of soldiers or another. Breathless, he reached his home, which was located in a village near Yerushalayim.

He collapsed onto a chair, but got up a moment later. "I must not remain dressed in the *bigdei kehunah*," the thought crossed his mind. "It is only permitted to wear these clothes in the Beis

---

1. Mishnah *Middos* 3:5.
2. Ibid., 5:4, *Tiferes Yisrael* #27.

HaMikdash."[3] Quickly and reverently he took off the special garments. He remembered that by wearing these clothes while not in the service of the Beis HaMikdah he was transgressing the prohibition of *shaatnez*, because the *avneit* was made from a mixture of wool and linen.[4] Normally a forbidden combination, it was only allowed to be worn while performing the *avodah*.[5] He stashed the clothes in his basement, hidden among a pile of rags.

Isamar stayed at home, waiting for developments. The distressing news reached the little village, and Isamar understood that the Beis HaMikdash had fallen into Greek hands. Pained and saddened, he remained holed up in his village, hoping to escape danger. For an entire year, he stayed *tahor*, waiting for the day the Beis HaMikdash would be back in Jewish hands and he could finally resume his *avodah* there.

On the twenty-fifth of Kislev, in the early afternoon, the good news reached the village: the Beis HaMikdash is back in our hands! Ecstatic, yet worried about the grim scene he might find in the Beis HaMikdash, Isamar took the *bigdei kehunah* from their hiding place and set out for Yerushalayim.

When he reached the city, he discovered that there was not a single pure Kohen around. Without hesitating, he went to the *Beis Din* near Har HaBayis and with one short sentence he moved them all to tears.

He said six little words, not more. "I am a Kohen, and I am *tahor*."

*　　　*　　　*

---

3. *Yoma* 69a.

4. Rambam, *Hilchos Klei HaMikdash* 8:1.

5. Ibid., 8:12.

Half an hour later, Isamar found himself standing in the *Heichal*(11), facing the iron Menorah(84) coated in tin.[6] It stood eighteen *tefachim* high,[7] its bowls were filled to the top with oil, half a *log* in each,[8] and next to it were three stone steps.[9]

The steps were found tossed in one of the chambers of the Beis HaMikdash. They were not *tamei* because they were made of stone and stone cannot become *tamei*.[10]

Isamar slowly climbed the steps, looking around with an ache in his heart. The *Heichal* was bare. There was no *Shulchan*(85) and no *Mizbeach*(83), and a simple iron Menorah stood in for the magnificent golden one. As always, two *parochos*(19) separated the *Heichal*(11) from the *Kodesh HaKodashim*(12).

With his voice trembling and with intense concentration, eyes heavenward, he began to recite the *berachah*. "*Baruch Atah Hashem, Elokeinu Melech HaOlam, asher kideshanu b'mitzvosav v'tzivanu l'hadlik neiros.*"[11] It was all he could do to steady his shaking hand and light the wicks, one after another. Seven pure lights were kindled, seven flames reflected in his sparkling eyes. He bowed and exited the *Heichal*.

*   *   *

A group of Jews stood in the Yerushalmi *beis ha-knesses* that had just reopened its doors that day. Between *Minchah* and *Maariv*, the *talmidei chachamim* who were present struck up a casual conversation.

---

6. *Avodah Zarah* 43a.

7. Rashi, *Shemos* 25:35.

8. *Menachos* 89a.

9. Mishnah *Tamid* 3:9.

10. Mishnah *Ohalos* 5:5.

11. Maran HaGaon Rav Chaim Kanievsky *shlita*.

*It was all he could do to steady his shaking hand
and light the wicks, one after another.*

"In a few minutes, Rav Avigdor, one of the Sages of the Sanhedrin, will be here to give us a *shiur*," said an older man whose
beard was still a distinctly red color. "Imagine! A *shiur* taught in
public! Just like that, out in the open, without fear!" His tone was
jubilant. "I hereby accept upon myself, *bli neder*, to attend the *shiur*
every day. Hashem has shown us so much kindness and we must
repay Him with at least a little extra effort!"

A thin man with an intense expression on his face shared his
thoughts with the group. "Isn't it interesting that the *avodah* of the
korbanos resumed specifically with the lighting of the Menorah?
Olive oil represents the pure wisdom of the Torah, which defeated
the impure Greek wisdom!"[12]

"A fascinating idea! The date that it took place also holds
special significance," added another man, known for his deep
insights.

"Really? What's so special about this day?"

"At the end of Kislev, hundreds of years ago, the construction
of the Mishkan was completed in the desert. The inauguration of
the Mishkan was not held on that day, though, because Hashem
commanded Moshe Rabbeinu to wait until Rosh Chodesh Nissan.[13] It seems that the month of Kislev finally received its due,
after all these years."[14]

"I heard that they made the Menorah(84) out of iron spits —
pointed metal rods used for grilling meat over a fire,"[15] added
Shimon, changing the subject slightly.

"That's not correct," responded the older man. "They made it
out of raw iron, not spits."

---

12. *Bnei Yissaschar*, Kislev 7.

13. *Midrash Tanchuma, Pekudei* 11.

14. *Bnei Yissaschar*, Cheshvan.

15. *Menachos* 28b.

"Interesting. Then why did people tell me it was made of spits?"

"They probably meant to say that since the Menorah has no *gevi'im, kaftorim* or *perachim*, its branches resemble spits."[16]

"What are they going to do tomorrow?" wondered a tall man. "It seems they only had enough oil for one day."

The older man looked up and lifted his hands. "Is Hashem's power limited?[17] Think for a minute. Yesterday, did it ever occur to you that today a Kohen would light the Menorah(84) in the *Heichal*? Yesterday, the city was still filled with Greeks, impurity, and an overpowering fear, and in an instant that's all gone! If Hashem wills it, then tomorrow we will also light the Menorah with pure oil!" Nods of agreement came from all sides.

The sight of the rav in the doorway sent all the men scurrying back to their places. Charged with emotion, they sat down in their seats and preparing to drink in words of Torah. For the first time in a long time, they would do so publicly, without fear.

*   *   *

In the *beis midrash* in Mount Moda'is, a *shiur* was taking place as well, but the boys in the class were having a hard time concentrating. The knowledge that they were going home tomorrow was so exciting, so mind-boggling, that Elkanah's words fell on deaf ears.

After attempting another sentence or two, he muttered something to himself decisively, and gently rolled up the scroll.

"When would you rather leave, tomorrow or the next day?" he asked, kissing the closed book of *Navi*.

"Tomorrow! Definitely tomorrow!" the children said, and erupted in excited chatter. They didn't even realize that the class had come to an abrupt end.

---

16. *Tosfos,* ibid., s.v. *shipudim.*
17. *Bemidbar* 11:23.

"Why does Rebbi want us to wait another day?" Sharp-minded Yedidya understood that Elkanah must have a good reason for asking.

"I thought you might want to participate in the building of the *Mizbeach*(7)," Elkanah replied, much to the boys' surprise.

"The building of the *Mizbeach*?!" they asked in disbelief.

"Us?" squealed Boaz, wide-eyed.

Elkanah smiled at their astonishment. "I'll explain," he said calmly. "This morning, the *Beis Din* in Yerushalayim issued a ruling that a new *Mizbeach* should be built to replace the one defiled by the Greeks.[18] If you'd like, you can help with this holy work."

"Yes! Yes! We want to!" The boys were ecstatic. Yehudah even started to jump up and down on the bench.

"So we won't go home tomorrow," Mahalalel said. "It's okay. We waited six months; we can wait one more day."

"But, one minute…" Cautious Naftali was not swept up in the excitement. "How can we help with the construction? We're not allowed to enter the *Ezras Kohanim*(6)!"[19]

Elkanah lifted a hand and the children quieted down. "A Yisrael may enter the *Ezras Kohanim* for the purpose of building the *Mizbeach*, but in any case, you'll help out in a different way. The stones for the *Mizbeach* are being taken from the Beis Kerem valley.[20] Digging stones from the earth is not an easy job. With Hashem's help, tomorrow, on the way home, we'll pass by that way and stay a while to help the workers with their job."

                    *   *   *

"Everyone is going home to a father and mother…" Reuven lay on the straw mattress, tears dripping from his eyes. "Tomorrow

---

18. *Avodah Zarah* 52b.

19. Mishnah *Keilim* 1:8.

20. Mishnah *Middos* 3:4.

every boy will go home and see his father. Only I won't see my father. My poor father was sold as a slave, and who even knows where he is and what's happening to him. Is he suffering? Are they beating him?" A shiver went through his body. He turned around to face the wall, and through his quiet sobs he began to recite *Tehillim*, pleading with Hashem from the depths of his heart to watch over his father.

At the time that his pure *tefillos* went up to the heavens, Reuven's father was already back in Eretz Yisrael, a free man. Reuven didn't know it, but he would see his father much sooner than he expected.

*   *   *

One week earlier, Binyamin's master summoned Augustus for an urgent meeting.

Augustus, as you'll recall, traveled to Tzidon and posed as a timber merchant, for the purpose of liberating Binyamin, Reuven's father, from slavery.

"I need your help," said the master, nervously smoothing out his cloak. "As a colleague, I'm sure you know that the number one rule for running a successful timber business is to provide merchandise on time, without any undue delays."

"Of course, of course," nodded Augustus, hoping the expression on his face was that of an experienced, knowledgeable timber merchant.

"This morning I ran into a serious problem. A few months ago, I signed a contract with a customer from Yerushalayim in which I guaranteed to provide him with two hundred high-quality cedar tree trunks. The final date of delivery is in ten days."

"Well, then, what's the problem?" Augustus twisted the ring on his finger with feigned indifference. "If you're traveling fast, you can get from here to Yerushalayim in three days. Let's say wagons loaded with wood move a little slower. Even so, it shouldn't take more than ten days!"

"That's exactly the problem! I don't have wagons!" The merchant stood up in frustration, and paced back and forth anxiously across the spacious parlor. "I had eight wagons ready and waiting in my courtyard. The hinges were oiled, the wheels were reinforced, and the horses were harnessed. This morning, soldiers showed up at my house with orders from the governor to confiscate the wagons for an unknown length of time.

"There's a revolt going on in Yerushalayim, and all resources, both public and private, are being requisitioned for war. The Greek army decided that I must contribute my wagons, and now I have a problem," concluded the Lebanese master, sinking into his chair.

"Your customers will understand that it's not your fault. You had a good reason for the delay," Augustus tried to reassure him.

"A good merchant doesn't look for excuses. He keeps his promises no matter what. I didn't invite you here so that you could offer me consolation. I want to hear some solid advice!" said the merchant in irritation.

Augustus thought for a moment.

"One minute," he said, as if he had just remembered something. "You have a Jewish slave here, don't you? What's his name?"

"Binyamin," answered the merchant impatiently. "But what does he have to do with this? I need to…"

Augustus cut him off. "You boasted about how clever he is. Call him here. Maybe he'll have a good idea."

During the short walk from the courtyard where he was trimming the grass to his master's house, Binyamin's lips whispered a prayer. His master had woken up that morning in a rotten mood, and he had tried to stay out of his way. The summons worried him, and he asked Hashem to spare him from his master's wrath.

"Good afternoon, Binyamin. How are you today?" He could hardly believe his ears, but his master's voice was positively friendly. In fact, it was so sweet it practically dripped honey. His master had never spoken to him that way before.

"*Baruch Hu u'varuch Shemo*," he replied, lifting his eyes in thanks to Hashem.

The merchant grimaced. "All right, we'll let it be. I need your advice. I must transport a timber delivery to Yerushalayim with the utmost urgency, and I have no wagons. Let's see you, smart Jew that you are, come up with a brilliant solution to this problem."

A *pasuk* from Tanach flashed through Binyamin's mind. "We will cut trees from Lebanon, as much as you need, and we will bring them to you as rafts on the Sea of Yaffo, and you will bring them up to Yerushalayim."[21] He remembered what Shlomo HaMelech did when he wanted to bring wood from Lebanon to build the Beis HaMikdash, and he answered simply, "Transport them by sea."

His master twisted his face in scorn. "Where will I get a boat big enough to hold two hundred tree trunks? It's wartime now, and all large ships have been pressed into the service of the military. My friend has a small boat, but it won't hold more than fifty trunks. Really! Can't you give me a better solution than that?"

"That's not what I meant," Binyamin clarified, ignoring the insult. "I was thinking of something much simpler than that. Tie the trees to each other with ropes to create rafts, just like King Shlomo did. Tie the rafts to your friend's boat, and then you can bring it all to Yerushalayim quickly and easily."

The timber merchant gaped at him, wide-eyed. "I hadn't thought of that! Your idea is brilliant in its simplicity." He clasped Binyamin on the shoulder, and turned to Augustus. "Now you understand why I won't sell him for all the money in the world. I'd have to be an idiot to lose a slave as smart as this!"

---

21. *II Divrei HaYamim* 2:15.

Chapter Nineteen
Song in the Cellar

The Lebanese timber merchant clapped his hands together in satisfaction. "Binyamin's idea is excellent! Just excellent! We'll take the wood by sea to the port of Yaffo and from there by wagon to Yerushalayim.

He thumped Augustus on the shoulder in an exaggerated gesture of friendship. "Tell me, do you plan to stay here longer, or have you finished your business already? Would you like to transport the timber for me? For payment, of course."

Thoughts filled Augustus's head in a disordered jumble. He paced back and forth on the luxurious carpet, weighing every aspect of the situation. On the one hand, he certainly had not finished his business in Lebanon. He didn't want to leave as long as Binyamin was still in captivity. On the other hand…yes, this was a good way out, a chance to escape.

The merchant breathed a sigh of relief when Augustus finally looked up and said, "I agree."

*　　　*　　　*

Three days later, two hundred tree trunks stood at the dock in the port, tied securely into rafts. Ten of the master's slaves, among them Binyamin, were sweating profusely as they lowered the rafts into the sea. The small sailboat was anchored near the shore, and the three rafts were tied to it with rope.

The slaves left, and Augustus, a bundle of nerves, engaged the master in a long conversation, making sure the merchant's back was to the sea. Binyamin, who was waiting for this moment, leapt into

the water, swam quickly towards the boat, and climbed up a ladder that was prepared for this purpose. Hunched over, he ran onto
the deck and then down into the belly of the ship. He counted two
cabins from the right and opened the door. As agreed, there was
a bed there draped in a long piece of fabric that reached the floor.
He lifted up the cover, crawled under the bed, and waited with a
pounding heart. Ten minutes later, the horn blared. Binyamin felt
a slight shake, and the boat left the
shallow waters of the port and
sailed out into the open sea.

The boat left the shallow waters of the port and sailed out into the open sea.

Two hours later, the Tzidoni merchant discovered that Binyamin was missing. He ran to the slaves' quarters and checked the shelf next to Binyamin's bed. As he suspected, it was empty. His tallis and tefillin were not there.

His shouts could be heard all over. "He escaped! Impudent fellow! Ingrate! I'll show him!" The merchant thought a little and then realized that Binyamin must be on the boat.

"He'll see! I won't give him up so easily! Pilos! Matthias!" Two servants hurried to appear before their master, trembling. "You're going right now! Ride as fast as you can! You must get there before him! In three days, the ship will anchor in Yaffo, and you'll be waiting for him there!" He laughed raucously. "You'd better bring him back here, no matter what! You've been duly warned!"

*   *   *

Binyamin sat on a soft feather pillow, breathing in the salty sea air and gazing at the sun slowly rising in the east.

He breathed in the taste of freedom, and an infinite gratitude spread throughout his every limb. *Baruch Hashem*, Augustus's plan had worked. The captain didn't suspect a thing. Augustus had informed him ahead of time that he would be bringing along an assistant.

At the sound of approaching footsteps, Binyamin opened his eyes. Augustus sat down on the chair next to him, looking at the escaped slave in satisfaction.

"How is to be free?" he asked.

"*Baruch Hashem*! '*Chasdei Hashem ki lo samnu* — Hashem's kindnesses never cease!'"[1] replied Binyamin, meaning every word.

"Now I can tell you how I got to you."

Binyamin turned his chair around, looking at his rescuer in

---

1. *Eichah* 3:22.

curiosity. How, in fact, did this man know him and why did he decide to save him?

Augustus sipped some water and began to speak. "In the past, I was a Tzedoki, and as soon as the Greeks entered Yerushalayim I became a *misyavein*. I landed a good job as the assistant to the Greek police chief in the holy city. But the shameful takeover of your house and the way you were sold into slavery disgusted me, and they were actually what inspired me to make a change in my life.

"I decided that at the first opportunity, I would leave Pelagios and try to liberate you. I secretly took the money that he received in exchange for your sale, and one day I got up and traveled to Tzidon. The rest you know, and now, with Hashem's help, we're here."

Augustus stood at the ship's railing, staring at the trail of foam the boat left in its wake.

Binyamin turned his head in amazement, groping for the right words. "There is no way I can ever thank you! Anything I say will be a pathetic attempt at expressing my gratitude."

Augustus waved his hand dismissively. Binyamin went on, a worried crease appearing on his forehead. "I don't think I'm out of danger yet, though. If I know my former master, he won't give in so easily. I'm nearly certain that his messengers will be waiting for me at the port of Yaffo."

The wheels in Augustus's head turned quickly. "I have an idea," he finally said, reconsidering it once again and deciding that it would work. "Tomorrow we'll pass by the port of Acco. I'll purchase a rowboat from the captain and you'll take it and row to shore. As far as I'm concerned, your master's men can wait in Yaffo forever…"

They shared relieved smiles, and Binyamin went down to his cabin, donned his tallis and tefillin, and davened *Shacharis* as a free man for the first time. Free! What a wonderful word!

As Reuven murmured words of *Tehillim* and begged Hashem

to bring back his father, Binyamin's feet touched solid ground. He bent over and kissed the golden sand, a mask of tears blurring his view of the city of Acco spread out in front of him.

After a few moments, he stood up, dusted off his clothes, and checked his pocket. Yes, the pouch containing fifteen hundred dinars was safe and sound. Binyamin and Augustus had argued about the money, each one insisting that it belonged to the other. In the end, they agreed that the money would be dedicated to the Beis HaMikdash when it returned to the hands of the Chashmonaim.

Binyamin took a room in a small, local inn that he was familiar with from his business trips. He had decided to spend the night in Acco. It was dangerous to travel after dark, and after all that he had been through, he didn't want to take any risks.

His bones ached from the boat ride, and the ceiling spun dizzily in front of his eyes. He could feel the rocking of the boat, as if he was still on board. He recited *Keriyas Shema* with immense gratitude and *kavanah*, and immediately fell into a deep sleep.

*   *   *

The evening of the twenty-sixth of Kislev spread its wings over the holy city of Yerushalayim.

In the *batei midrash*, candles cast their light all around. A sweet melody overflowed into the streets as throngs of people sat inside and learned Torah out loud, as if it were eleven o'clock in the morning instead of eleven o'clock at night. After being banned from studying Torah publicly for such a long time, the Jews found it impossible to part from the *sifrei Torah, Nevi'im* and *Kesuvim*. Stop learning and go to sleep? That seemed like a ridiculous waste of time.

In the *Beis Din*, as well, the *dayanim* sat on their chairs, summing up the day's activities. One of the elder Kohanim stood up and presented the next day's schedule.

"With Hashem's help, tomorrow morning, right after *Shacharis k'vasikin*, fifty workers will head out to the Beis Kerem valley. They'll arrive about three hours after sunrise and immediately begin digging stones from the ground. According to reports we've received, the demolition of the old *Mizbeach* should be finished at some point tonight. We've decided to dig a deep pit in the *Lishkas HaChosamos*(59) and place the stones of the old *Mizbeach* inside.[2]

"In addition, tomorrow we will be receiving long beams to make a wooden frame in which to cast the new *Mizbeach*(7).[3] I hope that within a day the first stage of the *Mizbeach*, the *Yesod*, will be completed.

The *av beis din* shot him a questioning look. "Have we ordered large enough quantities of all the materials we need?"

"Absolutely. The barrels of tar, lead, and lime that will be used to cast the *Mizbeach* should all arrive tomorrow morning."

The *av beis din* nodded his head in satisfaction and adjourned the meeting. "We'll reconvene tomorrow to discuss what else needs to be done to make new vessels for the Beis HaMikdash."

*　　　*　　　*

"Abba, it's late at night! I think you'd better stop now." Shmaryahu looked at his father with concern. "We can assemble the cedar wood for the *Shulchan* tomorrow! All the wood is already cut exactly to size, 'two *amos* long and one *amah* wide and one-and-a-half *amos* high.'"[4]

His father was so engrossed in his work that he didn't even hear what his son said. The table in front of him was strewn with wood pieces and tools and he was deep in concentration, hard at work building the *Shulchan*(85) for the *lechem ha-panim*. This

---

2. Mishnah *Middos* 1:6.

3. *Zevachim* 54a.

4. *Shemos* 25:23.

carpenter may not have had the *chochmah, binah,* and *da'as* (wisdom, insight, and knowledge) used in the creation of the world that Betzalel had when he built the original *Shulchan,*[5] but he still tried his best to think only holy thoughts while he was working.

"Abba, you've been working for ten hours straight," Shmaryahu pleaded. "Maybe you should go rest now and continue tomorrow. Please!"

Finally, the boy's words penetrated his father's thoughts. He lifted his deep blue eyes and looked at his son in consternation. "How can I stop?" he asked in all seriousness. He truly did not understand. "I'm not just building another piece of furniture. I am building the *Shulchan* that will stand in the house of Hashem! Come, Shmaryahu," he said forgivingly, "you must be very tired by now. Put your hand right here and I'll hammer. We'll be done in half an hour. Tomorrow, with Hashem's help, we'll get the gold we need to overlay the *Shulchan*![6] How fortunate we are to have been chosen for this holy task!"

His wrinkled face glowed, and with a look of sheer joy he went back to his work.

Way past midnight, the door to the carpentry shop was locked and father and son made their way through the empty alleys. The distant sound of singing reached their ears. They slowly walked up the street, father leaning on his son's arm. The song grew louder until they could tell which house it was coming from. They went right up to the window, which was close to the ground, and peered into the house's cellar. The voices were perfectly clear now.

"*Aromimcha Hashem ki dilisani v'lo simachta oyvai li* — I will exalt You, Hashem, for You have raised me up, and You have not allowed my enemies to rejoice over me."

---

5. *Shemos Rabbah* 48:4.

6. *Shemos* 25:24.

The song was being sung by dozens of men who were crowded into the cellar.

"Those must be the Leviyim practicing for the *Chanukas Ha-Bayis* that will be held in a few more days," the father explained knowingly.

"Why did they specifically choose these *pesukim*?" asked Shmaryahu, eyes glued to the incredible sight.

"These *pesukim* are from the *perek* of *Tehillim*[7] that begins with the words, 'A song for the inauguration of the House, by Dovid," his father said fondly. "How wonderful that I have a part in it, too! I don't know why I was given the *zechus* of building the *Shulchan*."

They listened raptly to the soft, sweet sound of singing.

"*Hashem Elokai shivati eilecha va'tirpa'eini* — Hashem, I cried out to You, and You healed me."

How fitting those words were for the times! Hashem, I cried out to you, during the Greek exile, and You healed me, through the Chashmonaim.[8]

The Leviyim sang in low voices so as not to wake the neighbors, but their deep emotion was apparent. "*Hashem he'elisa min she'ol nafshi chiyisani miyordi vor* — Hashem, You have brought my soul from the grave, You have revived me from my descent into the pit." The slow, soulful rhythm turned suddenly fast and upbeat. "*Zamru laShem chasidav v'hodu l'zecher kadsho* — Sing to Hashem, His devout ones, and give thanks to His holy Name." His devout ones — those are the sons of Matisyahu.

The Leviyim closed their eyes, and tapped their feet to the music. The melody was captivating, and soon the courtyard was filled with passersby who stopped to listen. Just two days ago

---

7. *Tehillim* 30.

8. *Midrash Tehillim*, ibid.

they had been hiding out in their homes from fear of their oppres-
sors, and now they could say Hashem's Name in public, proudly.
As if on their own, hands were linked inside each other and feet
lifted in dance.

"*Zamru laShem chasidav v'hodu l'zecher kadsho.*"

Chapter Twenty

The Miracle of the Oil Jug

E arly in the morning, Isamar, the Kohen who was *tahor*, appeared in the *Beis Din* at the entrance to Har HaBayis(44).

"Should I do *hatavas ha-neiros* this morning?" he asked the *dayanim*. "Chances are I won't be lighting the Menorah this evening. At the moment, we have no more pure oil. The question is, should I prepare the lights anyway?"

"Yesterday morning there didn't seem to be any chance, either, and look! Last night you lit the Menorah!" said one of the elder Kohanim with a touch of rebuke in his voice.

"We'll do our part and Hashem will do the rest," said the *av beis din*. "Go and prepare the lights."

"Normally, five lamps are prepared, and then the blood of the *Tamid* is thrown against two corners of the *Mizbeach*. After that, the other two lamps are prepared,"[1] said Isamar. "Today, there won't be a *korban Tamid*, so should I prepare all the lamps at the same time?"

After some deliberation, the answer came. "Despite the absence of the *Tamid*, *hatavas ha-neiros* should be done in two stages. Ideally, there should be a break between the two with an *avodah*

---

1. *Yoma* 33a.

performed in between.[2] Today, since there is nothing to do in between, you should prepare five lamps, wait half an hour, and then prepare the other two."

*   *   *

The Kohen entered the *Heichal* holding the *kuz*,[3] the vessel into which he would put the old wicks.[4] To his surprise, the lamps were still burning, illuminating the *paroches*(19) behind them.

"Interesting," he murmured to himself. "Usually, during the long winter nights, the oil is used up as soon as morning arrives, and when the Kohen comes to prepare the Menorah the lamps are already extinguished."[5]

He knew the relevant halachos very well, even though he only had the privilege of performing *hatavas ha-neiros* twice in his life. In the event that the lamps are still burning, the Kohen extinguishes five of them, removes the burnt wicks, and cleans out the oily residue. Then he pours in new oil and puts in new wicks.[6]

He climbed the stone steps, and when he peeked into the bowls, he got so dizzy he almost fell flat on the floor. The bowls were filled to the top with oil![7] It looked as though they had just been lit, when in fact they had been burning for over fourteen hours!

"It's a miracle! A miracle!" he whispered, as everything swam in front of his eyes and a tingle went down his spine. It took all of his self-control not to run outside and share the incredible news with everyone.

---

2. *Kesef Mishneh* on Rambam, *Hilchos Temidin u'Musafin* 3:16.
3. Mishnah *Tamid* 3:6.
4. Ibid., 3:9.
5. Rashi, *Shemos* 27:21.
6. Bartenura, Mishnah *Tamid* 3:9.
7. *Beis Yosef, Orach Chaim* 670 (the third answer).

"It's a miracle! A miracle!" he whispered.

"First, I must perform the mitzvah I came to do," he thought, taking a deep breath. The dizziness slowly ebbed. He extinguished five of the lamps, carefully removed the wicks, bent over, and deposited them in the *kuz* that rested on the second of the three steps.[8] Slowly and deliberately, he inserted five new wicks, and with legs trembling, he left the *Heichal*.

*   *   *

The *dayanim* were gripped with fear when they saw Isamar return to the *Beis Din*. His face was white and his hands wouldn't stop shaking.

"A miracle! A miracle!" he cried, collapsing into the first chair he saw.

"What happened? Tell us!" commanded the *av beis din*. All the *dayanim* stared at the Kohen, hearts pounding.

"I went into the *Heichal* to prepare the Menorah. The bowls are full of oil!" he whispered, hardly believing his own words.

"What do you mean?" The *dayanim* were confused. Had they understood correctly?

"Hashem loves us. Hashem is pleased with our actions! He wants us to light the Menorah again today!" He paused, took a deep breath, and continued, a bit calmer now. "From far, I could see that the lamps were still burning. I looked inside and was stunned to see that none of the oil was gone. It was as if the Menorah was just lit!"

The wonderful news spread throughout the entire city of Yerushalayim. A sense of love and consolation trickled into the people's hearts. How special it was to feel that Hashem desired their *avodah*! *Hodu laShem ki tov ki l'olam chasdo*!

*   *   *

---

8. Mishnah *Tamid* 3:9.

Until that moment, the leaders of the rebellion were not absolutely sure they had acted correctly. By revolting against the Greeks, they had placed the Jewish people in great danger, a danger that had not yet passed. They knew that the Greeks would not let themselves be defeated so easily. They would return to Yerushalayim, stronger and crueler than ever. On the other hand, they couldn't sit around with their arms folded any longer while Hashem's Name was trampled and disgraced for all to see. The desire to stand up for Hashem's honor pulsed through their veins, urging them to stand up and fight.

The miracle of the oil was like a loving smile from Above, like a shining star from *Shamayim*. It was as if Hashem was whispering to them, "You did the right thing, My sons. You gave Me *nachas*. I'm pleased with your actions."[9]

"It was specifically through olive oil, a symbol of the wisdom of Torah, that the miracle came about,"[10] the elder Kohanim whispered among themselves. "The holy Torah will prevail over the forces of *tum'ah*!"

"Our actions are pleasing to Hashem," said Reb Avigdor the *dayan* to his friend, in a voice choked with emotion. "Yesterday, a heavy weight rested on my chest. Maybe our decision to destroy the *Mizbeach* was incorrect. Perhaps we transgressed the prohibition of 'You shall not do so to Hashem, your God.' The miracle of the oil reassured me. I see it as a sign from Heaven that our decision was correct and proper."[11]

With a bounce in his step, the Kohen left the two-story house and headed for the Beis HaMikdash. Once again, he entered the *Heichal*, approached the Menorah, and did as they used to do in

---

9. *Al HaTeshuos*, p. 223.

10. *Menachos* 85b.

11. *Eishel Avraham* on *Megillas Ta'anis* (25 Kislev).

the times of Shimon HaTzaddik: he extinguished one lamp and replaced its wick. He left the western lamp burning; he would prepare it only later that evening, before lighting the Menorah. When he finished, he prostrated himself fully on the ground, his heart overflowng with gratitude to Hashem. Then he left, taking the *kuz* with him. He sidestepped the now-empty spot where the *Mizbeach* was supposed to be, and put the wicks on the ground where the ashes of the *Mizbeach* were ordinarily placed.[12] He knew that very soon they would miraculously be swallowed up into the ground.[13]

*   *   *

Towards the afternoon of the twenty-sixth of Kislev, Elkanah and his students arrived at the Beis Kerem valley. The workers' voices and the cries of the foreman could be heard from a distance and guided them to the work site. When they got close enough, they could see two wagons standing there.

"You came to help?" the foreman welcomed them with a broad grin. "Wonderful! We can use more pairs of hands!"

"Give the children exact instructions, please," requested Elkanah.

The boys stood in a wide circle around the foreman, who rubbed his hands on his clothes, trying to wipe away the thick layer of dust that encrusted them. "In order for a stone to be used for the *Mizbeach*, it must meet two requirements," he began. "One, it must be whole, without any breaks or cracks. Two, it cannot have touched iron.[14] That's why we came here, to Beis Kerem. Here, you can find stones that meet the description in the *pasuk*: 'You shall build the *Mizbeach* of Hashem out of whole

---

12. Mishnah *Tamid* 1:4.
13. *Yoma* 21a.
14. Mishnah *Middos* 3:4.

stones.'[15] In order to fulfill the second requirement, we dig into the ground using wooden tools, and we dig deep, to find stones that have never been touched by a human hand, let alone an iron utensil. This is also written in the Torah: 'When you make for Me a *Mizbeach* of stones, do not build them of hewn stones, for you will have raised your sword upon it and desecrated it.'[16] Once iron has touched stones, they are no longer fit to be used for the *Mizbeach*."

The foreman looked at the white stone hills that surrounded them and then back at the boys. "You'll notice that even the wagons we have here to transport the stones to Yerushalayim are made completely from wood. No iron may come in contact with the stones at any point in time."

"Why is that?" Naftali wanted to know.

"The *Mizbeach* was created to lengthen a person's life, through the *korbanos*, which atone for his sins. Iron, on the other hand, shortens a person's life, because it is used to make weapons. It is not fitting that iron which shortens life should be associated with the *Mizbeach* which lengthens life."[17] The explanation was so interesting that the boys didn't even notice the gusts of wind blowing through the valley.

Elkanah had something to add as well. "The *Mizbeach* brings peace between Bnei Yisrael and their Father in Heaven, therefore it cannot come in contact with iron, which cuts, separates, and harms.[18] Listen carefully, boys!" he cried, his voice echoing powerfully between the silent hills. "Stones are inanimate objects that don't see, hear, or speak. Yet because they bring peace, the

---

15. *Devarim* 27:6.

16. *Shemos* 20:22.

17. Mishnah *Middos* 3:4.

18. Rashi, *Shemos* 20:23.

Torah does not allow us to harm them with iron. How much more so are we guaranteed that a person who makes peace between man and his fellow will come to no harm!"

The foreman was visibly pleased with Elkanah's words, but the children were growing restless and it was time to start working. "All right, boys! Let's go! Five of you will join those workers over there, and the rest of you will dig right here. Your work should be done with a sense of responsibility and seriousness. This is not just any construction job. You are preparing stones for the *Mizbeach*!"

After two hours of hard work, with no breaks and almost no conversation, the boys sat down to rest under a tree. With a sense of satisfaction, they looked at the wagons which, together with the other workers, they had managed to fill.

A cloud of dust rose up behind them. Two empty wagons had returned from Yerushalayim, bearing the latest good news.

"Hashem performed a great miracle for us!" the wagon drivers said in excitement. "Yesterday, they were able to light the Menorah with pure oil that they found in the Beis HaMikdash. And this morning…it was incredible…when the Kohen went in to prepare the lamps, he saw that they were still burning and were still full of oil!"

Cries of amazement were heard all around. Some of the listeners rubbed their eyes, and not because there was dust in them…

"Elkanah, is that you?" came a cry of surprise. "I haven't seen you in months! I was afraid you'd been caught or exiled or worse…" The worker, a friend of Elkanah, was thrilled to see him.

"*Baruch Hashem*, none of those things happened to me. I spent a wonderful six months in a cave, in the company of these boys." He filled his friend in on what had transpired the last few months. "We stopped off here on our way home, in order to take part in the building of the new *Mizbeach*," he concluded his story.

A look of protest crossed his friend's face. "I must object. I think you may have made a mistake! The halachah clearly states that we do not interrupt children from their Torah learning even to build the Beis HaMikdash![19] The truth is that I never understood this halachah until now. Since when are young children involved in building the Beis HaMikdash? But now I see it in front of my own eyes. Young boys digging stones for the new *Mizbeach!*"

"*Yasher koach* for pointing out my error!" Elkaah thanked him warmly. "That halachah completely slipped my mind. I'll correct my mistake right now!"

---

19. *Shabbos* 119b.

Chapter Twenty-One

Preparing the Lamps

It was a quiet afternoon. A light breeze blew in through the arched windows, and sunlight danced off the marble floor of the shul in Beis Kerem, casting colorful sparks in every direction. Aside from the children, there were a number of elderly men and one boy learning with his father.

"How did you feel when you were digging the stones for the *Mizbeach*?" Elkanah threw out the question with a smile, waiting for the deluge of answers which quickly came.

"It felt great!"

"Uplifting!"

A special *zechus*!"

"So moving!"

"Thrilling!"

The boys' answers reflected the sense of satisfaction and importance that the work had given them.

"I'm happy you felt that way," their *rebbi* said, his gaze turning serious. "Even though I had good intentions, I erred in the halachah. You all know that the world exists in the merit of your Torah,[1] and therefore, 'we do not interrupt children from their Torah learning even to build the Beis HaMikdash.'

---

1. *Shabbos* 119b.

"When you were working on the stones, you probably felt that you were doing something important, something with a purpose. And of course, digging up stones for the *Mizbeach* is important! You should know, though, that when you're learning Torah you are doing something even more important and more beneficial than building the *Mizbeach*!"

He paused, letting his words sink in. Then he spoke again, this time in a voice tinged with nostalgia. "Today's lesson will probably be our last one together. Tomorrow, with Hashem's help, you'll be home!"

There were excited smiles all around. "For today's class, I chose a topic that's on everyone's mind: *hadlakas neiros.*" The boys leaned forward with interest, listening to every word. "Every day in the Beis HaMikdash, certain Menorah-related activities are performed. In the morning, *hatavas he-neiros* in done[2] in two stages,[3] and in the evening the Menorah is lit."[4]

"What's *hatavas he-neiros*? Does that mean they polish the Menorah?"

"No," Elkanah answered, hiding a smile. "*Hatavah* means cleaning and preparing.[5] In the morning, a Kohen takes out the old wicks and cleans out the remaining oil in the bowls on top of the Menorah. Then he puts new wicks in and fills up the bowls with oil,[6] but the Menorah is not lit. In the evening, when the afternoon *korban Tamid* is brought, the Kohen lights the wicks and they burn until morning."

"Is it true that the *ner ma'aravi*, the wick in the western bowl,

---

2. *Shemos* 30:7.

3. *Yoma* 33a.

4. *Shemos* 30:8.

5. Rashi, *Shemos* 30:7.

6. Mishnah *Tamid* 3:9.

burns all the time, day and night?"[7] asked Yedidya, shifting his position on the upholstered chair.

"It *was* true," Elkanah partially confirmed. "It was a miracle that happened every night, but it only lasted until the end of the era of Shimon HaTzaddik, who was the Kohen Gadol about a hundred and fifty years ago. This light was a testament to the fact that the *Shechinah* was found in Bnei Yisrael's midst.[8] It was an incredible sight to see how the western lamp continued to burn even though it had exactly the same amount of oil as the other lamps had, an amount that was sufficient to last through the long winter nights. Yet this lamp still burned throughout the entire next day. In the evening, right before lighting the Menorah, they would extinguish it and immediately light it again, together with the other six lamps.[9]

"My father once told me that the Menorah is positioned parallel to the width of the Beis HaMikdash, from north to south,"[10] said Reuven, wincing in pain at the thought of his beloved father.

Elkanah noticed it and hurried to distract him. "Your father was right. But what does that have to do with our discussion?"

"Well, if the lamps are positioned between north and south, then they're all equally close to the west.[11] So why is only one lamp called the 'western light'?"

"An excellent question!" Elkanah complimented him, gazing out at the view of the Beis Kerem valley from the window. "In fact, the answer is astounding in its simplicity. The western lamp is the middle light! It is the only one whose wick faces the west.

---

7. *Yoma* 39a.

8. *Shabbos* 22b.

9. Bartenura, Mishnah *Tamid* 3:9.

10. Rambam, *Hilchos Beis HaBechirah* 3:12.

11. *Menachos* 98b.

The wicks of the other six lamps face the middle lamp, as indicated in the *pasuk*, '…the seven lamps shall shine toward the main shaft of the Menorah.'"[12]

Mahalalel straightened out the embroidered tablecloth that covered the long, narrow table. "Why is it that the wicks face inward, as opposed to a normal lamp that spreads light outward?"

Elkanah sipped some water before answering. "There is actually a very special reason for that. It's so that people won't say that Hashem needs the light of the Menorah.[13] An ordinary lamp is used to chase away darknes and light up the surroundings. But the Beis HaMikdash is the House of Hashem, and Hashem doesn't need our light. The purpose of lighting the Menorah is to fulfill the mitzvah of Hashem, not to light up the room. In order to get that message across, the flames face inward."

"Rebbi said the lights are prepared in two stages," recalled Yossi. "How exactly is that done?"

"Thank you for reminding me. I wanted to discuss that further," said Elkanah. "The two stages are performed within a short time of each other. The first is done in the morning, before the *korban Tamid* is slaughtered. In this stage, the Kohen prepares five lamps. The second stage is done before the *ketores* is offered, when the Kohen prepares the remaining two lamps."[14]

"I don't understand!" A perplexed Yossi stood up, unwittingly dragging the tablecloth along with him. "Can't all the lights be prepared at the same time? Why is it divided into two?"

Elkanah got up and rearranged the tablecloth, which was trailing a bit on the floor. "The *pasuk* says, 'In the morning, in the

---

12. *Bemidar* 8:2.
13. Rashi, ibid.
14. *Yoma* 33a.

morning, when he prepares the lamps.'[15] Since the word *'ba-boker,'* in the morning, is written twice, the Sages understood that the preparation of the lights should be divided into two 'mornings'; that is, two stages."

"Then why divide it into five lamps and two lamps?" Naftali wondered aloud.

"Yeah, why?" the other boys echoed.

"Why not do six and then one?" Boaz's eyebrows shot up in curiosity.

"Or maybe five and two, but in the reverse order, first two and then five?" posited Zevulun.

"I see that you're slowly becoming real *talmidei chachamim!*" Elkanah praised them, raising his voice above the sound of theirs. "Listen well; the answer is the same for all your questions. The *pasuk* says, *'b'heitivo es ha-neiros* — when he prepares the **lamps**, in plural, teaching us that during each stage of preparation at least two lamps must be prepared. The Kohen prepares as many lamps as possible during the first stage, reserving the minimum amount — two — for the second stage."[16]

"What happens if the Kohen comes to prepare the lamps and he finds them still burning?" asked Yedidya. At the sight of his friends' questioning glances, he explained. "That could happen in the summer, when the nights are short and the oil doesn't get used up before morning.[17] It also happened this morning, miraculously."

"Let's take it one step at a time, so you'll understand what the Kohen does in every possible situation. We'll start with a case where the Kohen enters the *Heichal* and discovers that all the

---

15. *Shemos* 30:7.

16. *Yoma* 33b.

17. Bartenura, Mishnah *Menachos* 9:3.

lamps are extinguished already. In this case, he prepares five of them, and lights the other two."[18]

Three boys jumped up at once. "Lights them? Why?"

"Boys, let me continue. I promise that by the end you'll understand everything." The boys quieted down, and Elkanah took advantage of the silence and went on. "The Kohen would do that so that there would be a clear distinction between the two stages; it would be obvious because five lamps were extinguished and two were lit."[19]

Naftali's sharp mind grasped the problem instantly and he waved his hand in the air. "Since the two lamps went out, you can't light them without preparing them first and putting in more oil; so that means the Kohen is really preparing all seven lamps at the same time!"

"An excellent observation. In fact, the Kohen does prepare those two lamps before he lights them, but in a different way than the first five. The Kohen just removes the ash on the burnt tip of the wick and pulls the wick up a little. This treatment allows the lamp to burn for a few minutes, because the wick can then use up the little bit of oil remaining in the bowl.

"There is another possible scenario, in which the Kohen comes to the Menorah and finds all the lamps still burning. In this case, he extinguishes five, prepares them, and leaves the other two lit until he returns a little later to prepare them.[20] In the days of Shimon HaTzaddik he would prepare just one of the two and let the western lamp burn until evening."

Elkanah leaned on the window and continued. "The fire for lighting the Menorah is taken from the *Mizbeach*. In the times of

---

18. Mishnah *Tamid* 3:9.

19. Bartenura, ibid., s.v. *matz'an*.

20. Ibid., s.v. *u'matza*.

Shimon HaTzaddik, there was no need to take fire from the *Miz-beach*, because they could use the light of the western lamp which was always burning. After they lit the other six lamps from that fire, they would extinguish the western lamp and relight it with fire taken from one of the other lamps."

*   *   *

There was an unusual amount of traffic near one of the houses in Yerushalayim. Jews walked down the street, stood next to the house, waited a few minutes, and went on their way, slightly wet.

Before the Greeks came to power, people would come to that house to be purified. Now the house was thoroughly cleaned out and ready to be used for that purpose once again. Inside, next to the window facing the street,[21] stood a Jew who was *tahor*. He dipped a bundle of hyssop in water mixed with the ashes of a *parah adumah* and sprinkled it on the people who stood outside the window. This special water is called in the Torah "*mei chatas*."

The Yisraeli standing inside the house did his job with great devotion. He stood at his post for hours, loyally fulfilling this important mission.

Any Jew who became *temei meis* would come there beginning from the third day of his *tum'ah*. After the *mei chatas* touched his skin, he waited four days. In the second stage of his purification, the special water would be sprinkled on him again. Then, after immersing in the mikveh, he was no longer *temei meis*.[22]

On the twenty-sixth of Kislev, the sprinkler had hardly any work to do at all. Very few Jews came to be purified. The sprinkler took advantage of his free time to learn Torah. He knew that tomorrow, the twenty-seventh of Kislev, he would not have a moment's

---

21. Mishnah *Parah* 12:4.
22. *Bemidbar* 19:19.

*He dipped a bundle of hyssop in water mixed with the ashes of a parah adumah
and sprinkled it on the people who stood outside the window.*

rest. "Tomorrow is the third day since the war on Yerushalayim," he thought to himself. "Anyone who became *tamei* in battle on that day and wants to become *tahor*, can come tomorrow for the first stage of purification. I'll definitely have my hands full."

*   *   *

After a good night's sleep, Binyamin woke up, davened *Shacharis*, and ate a simple but nourishing breakfast. He bought a fast-running horse in the market for one hundred gold dinars — perhaps not a bargain but certainly a fair price. Binyamin mounted the horse and briefly considered which way to go. He could ride down the main highway, all along the coast, pass Yaffo, and then continue on to Yerushalayim. That route was quick and convenient, but Binyamin was afraid that he might meet up with his master's servants, and that was something he wanted to avoid at all costs.

He pulled on the horse's reins, directing them to a longer route, one that crossed the Lower Galilee. "Hopefully, I'll be home within three days," he murmured to himself, deeply inhaling the refreshing scent of winter and taking in the beautiful, familiar landscapes of his homeland.

He rode all day with stopping, except for short breaks to rest and daven. Before nightfall, he found an inn, where he was informed of the happy tidings of the liberation of Yerushalayim from enemy hands.

"Thank You, Hashem!" he said quietly, his eyes flooded with tears of joy. "I no longer have to be scared of that Greek commander who stole my house! How can I repay You for all the kindness You've done for me?"

Chapter Twenty-Two
Reuven Comes Home

T he morning of the twenty-seventh of Kislev dawned over a land that was slowly recovering from the ravages of war. The sun's rays carried good news: a miracle once again! For the second time, the Kohen had come to prepare the lamps and found them still burning, the bowls brimming with oil. This miracle held deep meaning for the long-suffering Jews. They saw it as a caress from the merciful hand of Hashem, Who loved them for remaining devoted to Him despite all the hardships.

*   *   *

In the *Azarah*, construction of the new *Mizbeach* was well underway. The *Yesod* was completely finished. Inside a wooden frame that measured thirty-two by thirty-two *amos* and one *amah* high, they placed the stones that had been dug up from the Beis Kerem valley. On top of these they poured a boiling hot mixture of tar, lime, and lead.[1] When the mixture cooled and dried, the wooden frame was removed and the builders got ready for the next phase of construction, which would take place on top of the rock-hard *Yesod*.

The *Sovev*(96) was built the same way, but its measurements were different. This time, the wooden beams formed a frame that was thirty by thirty *amos*, and five *amos* high. Stones were coming in at a brisk pace and the work was progressing nicely.

After much hard work, the *Shulchan*(85) and the *Mizbeach*

---

1. *Zevachim* 54a.

197

How the Mizbeach
Was Built

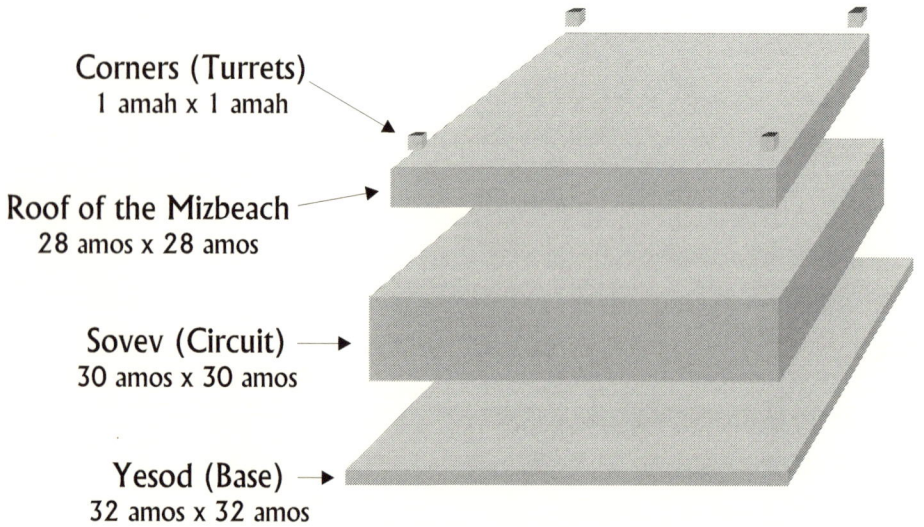

Corners (Turrets)
1 amah x 1 amah

Roof of the Mizbeach
28 amos x 28 amos

Sovev (Circuit)
30 amos x 30 amos

Yesod (Base)
32 amos x 32 amos

The Mizbeach and Its Ramps

HaZahav(83) were ready as well. Both of them were overlaid in gold, which had been very difficult for the Chashmonaim to find. There was no gold left for the Menorah, and with a heavy heart they accepted that they would have to continue with the iron one coated in tin that they were now using.

"As soon as we can, we'll build a silver Menorah," they promised themselves. "When things get even better, we'll build a magnificent golden Menorah with all its *kaftorim, perachim* and *gevi'im.*"[2]

*   *   *

It was a dusty bunch that quickly made its way through the narrow alleys. Elkanah and his students had finally arrived in Yerushalayim. Now, Elkanah went with them from house to house, safely delivering each boy to his parents, faithfully returning the precious treasures they had entrusted to him.

Inside the homes, the reunions were emotional. Parent gazed at the children who had grown beyond recognition, and they couldn't get enough of them.

"Six months in that cave really made them much more mature," Elkanah told his own family after the initial excitement of their reunion had subsided somewhat. He sat in the kitchen, inhaling the warm aromas of home, surrounded by family members listening to his tale. "The challenges we faced really strengthened them, and they are very serious young men. They love learning and they understand things in depth. It was an absolute pleasure to learn with them! It wasn't an easy time, for me or for them, but it was worth it. They really turned into *talmidei chachamim*!

"We made up to continue learning together here in Yerushalayim, starting tomorrow. We just can't part from each other. The time we spent together created a bond that runs very deep."

*   *   *

---

2. *Menachos* 28b.

With heavy steps and head down, Reuven entered the familiar courtyard. The gate creaked, and he saw his mother's face in the window.

"Reuven!" In an instant, she was outside, hugging and kissing him. They entered the house together. "My Reuven! I'm so happy to see you!" She smiled at him through her tears. "I hardly recognize you!"

"Ima, I can see that something is bothering you."

She sighed deeply and her face crumpled. "You're right. I'm worried about Abba," she said, confiding her troubles in her oldest son.

"Ima, everything is going to be all right," he comforted her, even though deep down he shared the exact same worry. "You'll see. Just like Hashem made a miracle for all of *Klal Yisrael*, He will make us our own personal miracle, too."

"Amen," whispered Reuven's mother, murmuring words of *Tehillim* as she wiped away hot tears.

A minor commotion and scraping sounds outside on the street drew their attention. Reuven drew the curtain aside and peered through the window, elated to see a familiar sight.

Streetcleaners were walking around with large sacks, thoroughly combing, as they did every day, every cobblestone and every crack, collecting every bit of dirt to ensure that there would not be even a lentil-sized bone of one of the eight *sheratzim* (like a mouse or a weasel) on the street, which could cause people to become *tamei*.[3]

"Hey!" cried Reuven. "That big idol that was here on the end of our street! It's gone!"

"Yes, *baruch Hashem*. The city is free of idols now," said his mother. "You weren't here two days ago. Everyone who could, lent a hand, and within a few hours there was not a single idol

---

3. *Bava Metzia* 26a, with *Tosfos* s.v. *asuyin*.

left in the city. They were all smashed to bits and the pieces were sent to rot in the Dead Sea."

"There's a new *beis midrash*, too!" Reuven's little brother piped up from his perch on the window sill. "The Greeks' big giant stadium was turned into a *beis midrash*! My friend Shimmy told me!"

Reuven stroked his cheek lovingly, and a sense of peace filled his heart. It was good to be home.

*   *   *

By now, the temporary *Beis Din* had twenty-three *dayanim*, as required of a minor Sanhedrin.[4]

"I hope and pray," said the *av beis din* at the opening of their first session, "that the day is not far when the Great Sanhedrin, made up of seventy-one *gedolei ha-dor*,[5] will once again sit in the *Lishkas HaGazis*(53)."[6]

One of the Kohanim informed the *dayanim* that there was not enough money to purchase *korbanos tzibbur*. The Greeks had completely emptied the *Lishkas HaShekalim*(71) and there were no funds left for *korbanos*.

"We'll send a crier around announcing that we are collecting *machatzis ha-shekel*," said the *av beis din*. "After all, this year we did not have the usual collection which is held every year before Nissan."[7]

He stood up to dictate the wording of the announcement to the scribe but was interrupted by the entrance of two Jews. The two men explained that before the war, they had lived on the second floor of adjacent houses with a narrow street separating their homes. When the Greek persecution began, they abandoned

---

4. *Sanhedrin* 2a.

5. Mishnah *Middos* 5:4.

6. *Sanhedrin* 2a.

7. Mishnah *Shekalim* 1:1.

their houses and escaped to the mountains in order to continue keeping mitzvos. Upon their return, they found that the Greeks had invaded their homes and built a large porch which connected the two second-floor dwellings. Now they wanted to know how they should divide the porch between them.

"One moment," said the *av beis din*, wrinkling his brow. "To decide a question of monetary matters, you only need a *beis din* of three judges,[8] not twenty-three like we have here. In any case, it seems to me that there is really no question at all."

"Why?"

"As I understand, the porch is built above the street. Is that correct?"

"Yes," the replied. They had no idea what he was getting at.

"If so, I hate to disappoint you, but you have to take it down."

The first neighbor's eyes lit up with understanding. "The halachah is that in Yerushalayim one may not build a porch that extends out into the street![9] How could we have forgotten?!"

"Well, then there's nothing for us to discuss," agreed the second neighbor. "But who will pay for the demolition of the porch?"

"*Beis Din* will take it down for you at public expense."

A few minutes after the two satisfied neighbors left *Beis Din*, the crier also left to spread his important message to all the residents of Yerushalayim.

*   *   *

"Ima, do you know…" Reuven was about to say something when his little brother shushed him.

"Shh…Reuven, there's a crier!"

The crier's voice grew louder and louder until they could hear him clearly.

---

8. *Sanhedrin* 2a.

9. *Bava Kamma* 82b.

"On the instructions of *Beis Din,* all men above the age of bar mitzvah should donate the half-shekel as soon as possible. In addition, all residents must be careful to observe the Sages' special edicts concerning the city of Yerushalayim: Do not make furnaces in the city! Do not extend beams and porches over the public domain! Do not raise chickens and do not make garbage dumps! *Beis Din* requests that everyone observe these decrees and correct that which needs correcting."

Throngs of Jews began streaming to the Shofar-chest(76) where the *machatzis ha-shekel* was deposited.[10] Things were going well, and *Beis Din* was pleased with the latest developments.

*   *   *

The door to the deliberations room was closed. The atmosphere was heavy as the *dayanim* discussed the matter of *Mishmeres* Bilgah.

Beis Din had already heard from two reliable witnesses about the offense of Miriam the daughter of Bilgah and the way she disgraced the *Mizbeach.*

"A serious misdeed like that cannot be allowed to pass in silence," said a severe-looking *dayan.*

"Her actions were indeed shameless and shocking, but she's left the country already, together with her Greek husband. There's no way we can punish her at all."

"The punishment will be meted out to her father's family," said the first *dayan.*

"Why is her father accountable for his daughter's appalling behavior?" wondered another.

"A child talking in the street repeats what he heard at home! If her home hadn't had an atmosphere of degradation and mockery

---

10. Mishnah *Shekalim* 6:5.

towards the *Mizbeach*, she never would have dared behave the way she did."

Another *dayan* confirmed his words. "I agree with you. Even more so, in my opinion the extended Bilgah family should be punished because 'Woe to a wicked person, and woe to his neighbor.'"

The *dayan* sitting at the far end of the table objected. "But they didn't do anything wrong! Why should they suffer the consequences of something they had nothing to do with?"

The *av beis din* was firm. "We must make some kind of distinction between the *mishmeres* of Bilgah and the other *mishmaros*, so that everyone will recognize the severity of the deed and understand that the extended family is responsible for the actions of individuals within the family. The punishment will be a constant reminder for every single Jew to stand guard and protect his family, and to rebuke any family member who transgresses the mitzvos of the Torah."

"There will be three punishments!" The *av beis din* announced the court's decision as the scribe's hand flew over the parchment, recording every word. "One: *Mishmeres* Bilgah will receive its share of the *lechem ha-panim* in the southern part of the *Azarah*. Even though the incoming *mishmar* receives its portion in the northern part of the *Azarah*, which is more important and prestigious, and the outgoing *mishmar* receives its portion in the southern part of the *Azarah*, the family of Bilgah will always receive its share in the southern part, whether it is the Shabbos that they are leaving or the Shabbos that they are arriving.

"Two: the *Taba'as* of the *mishmeres* will be locked."

In the *Beis HaMitbachayim*(8) there were twenty-four *Taba'os*(77), rings used to secure the animals before slaughter. The *Taba'as* of the Bilga family would be permanently fixed to the floor, with no possibility of opening it. The Kohanim of the *mishmeres* would be forced to use the rings of other *mishmaros*.

"Three: their 'window' will be sealed."

The Punishments for Mishmeres Bilgah

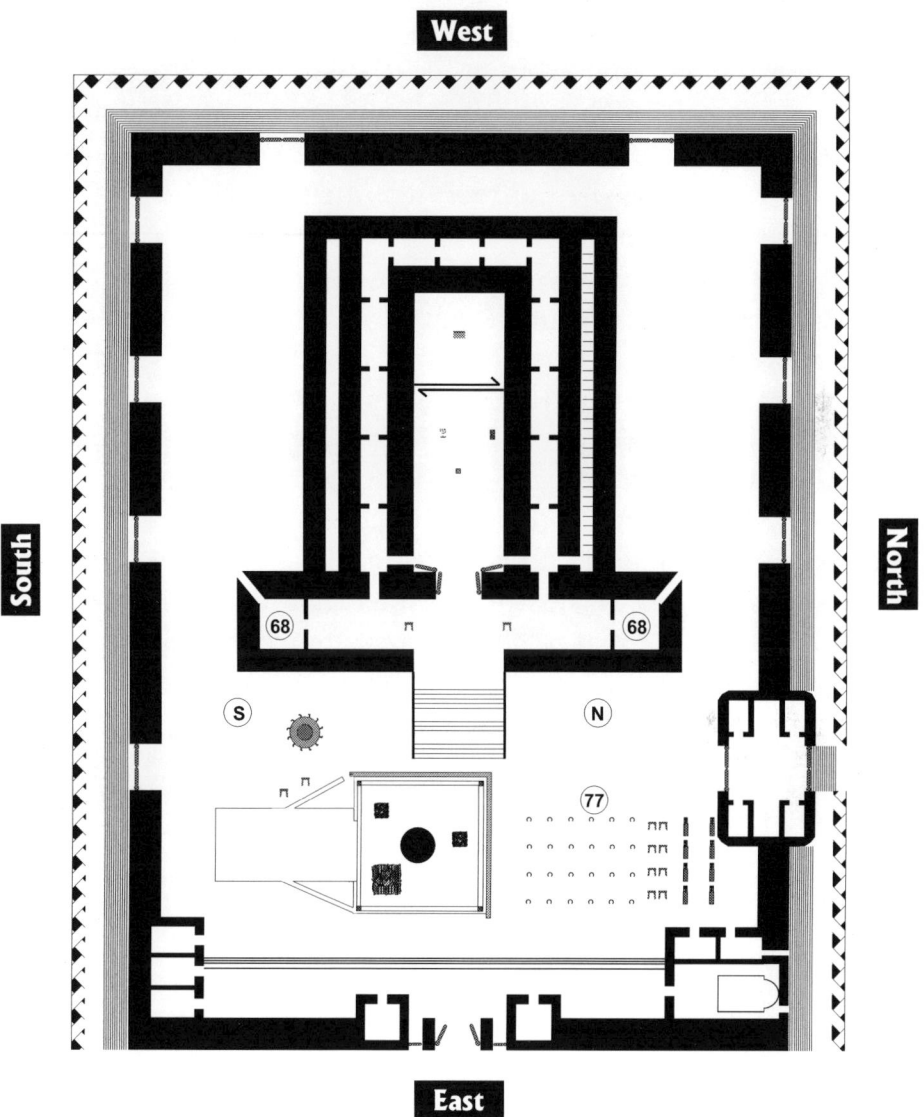

West

South

North

East

N Northern part of the *Azarah*   68. Knives Chambers

S Southern part of the *Azarah*   77. Rings to secure the animals for slaughter

Their special niche in the *Beis HaChalifos*, the Knives Chamber(68) — where the Kohanim kept their slaughtering knives — would be closed up.[11]

*   *   *

The night of the thirtieth of Kislev came and went and the moon was not seen. No witnesses had come all day, so the month of Kislev was declared a full month of thirty days.

The next day, on the evening of the first of Teves, a special *seudah* was held to publicize the *ibbur ha-chodesh*, the addition of another day to the month.[12] This meal of bread and legumes (like peas or beans), with at least ten Jews in participation, was held on the evening of Rosh Chodesh every time the previous month was *malei* — thirty-days long.

All last year, this *seudah* had been held underground. This time, on Rosh Chodesh Teves, the crowd was larger than expected. Tzedokim and Baitosim came, and there were even *misyavnim* in attendance. The miracles that came in quick succession and the inspiration that filled the streets touched their hearts. An extinguished spark deep inside them was rekindled, and they began to search for the way back home.

---

11. *Sukkah* 56b.
12. *Sanhedrin* 70b.

Chapter Twenty-Two

The King Comes Home

T here was a chill in the pre-dawn air. Even before the sun came up, a steady stream of people made its way in the direction of the Beis HaMikdash. The procession began slowly, with just a few indviduals, but it quickly turned into a river of humanity. Thousands filled the alleyways, trembling as they walked, and not just because of the cold. They were filled with excitement and emotion. Today, on the third of Teves, the *avodah* of the *korbanos* would resume. It was almost a year since *korbanos* had been offered in the Beis HaMikdash.

The areas under the gates of Har HaBayis(25–28) were filled with shoes.[1] Because of the Torah's commandment to fear Hashem's sanctuaries,[2] the people walked around the area of the Beis Mikdash barefoot.[3] That way, their bodies connected to the holy ground, a connection which brought them to *taharah*, spiritual growth and even a deeper understanding of Torah. A person who had difficulty mastering a certain topic in the Torah could sense that stepping directly on the floor of the Beis HaMikdash caused his mind to open up and his brain to understand things in a new way.[4]

Those who entered the *beis ha-knesses* on Har HaBayis discovered that it had been cleaned and refurbished. Its walls were

---

1. Talmud Yerushalmi, *Pesachim* 7:12.
2. *Vayikra* 19:30, 26:2.
3. Rambam, *Hilchos Beis HaBechirah* 7:1–2.
4. *Ye'aros Dvash*, drush 11.

freshly whitewashed and the *Aron Kodesh* was filled with *sifrei Torah, Nevi'im* and *Kesuvim*.[5]

*   *   *

Next to the *Soreg*(14), the low wall that separated Har HaBayis(1) from the *Cheil*(2),[6] two new, clearly lettered signs were hung to replace the old ones that had been destroyed. In both *Lashon Ha-Kodesh* and Greek, the sign informed the people that entry to the *Cheil* was forbidden to Gentiles, and to Jews who were *temei meis*.[7]

This stone, engraved with Greek lettering, was found in an archeological dig on the Temple Mount. It says: "A non-Jew may not enter past the partition that encircles the Beis HaMik-dash into the surrounding courtyard. Violators will be put to death."

Leviyim were posted along the *Soreg*(14) to remind all visitors that they must comply with the Sages' new decree — to bow down opposite the places that the Greeks had broken and breached the *Soreg*, in order to thank Hashem for the downfall of Greece.[8] To their delight, no one needed a reminder. The people's gratitude overflowed naturally, and with a sense of uplift, they prostrated themselves, arms and legs outstretched,[9] toward the Beis HaMikdash.

---

5. Rashi, *Yoma* 68b, s.v. *beis ha-knesses*.

6. Mishnah *Middos* 2:3.

7. Mishnah *Keilim* 1:8.

8. Mishnah *Middos* 2:3.

9. *Tiferes Yisrael*, ibid.

The people prostrated themselves, arms and legs outstretched,
toward the Beis HaMikdash.

Near the *Soreg* stood an adult and a child who appeared to be father and son. The adult was careful not to get jostled amidst the crowd, while the boy stood at a distance from him, gazing at him with shining eyes.

"Reuven, my precious son, it's a shame for you to stay here with me," said Binyamin, who had just returned home the day before yesterday and hadn't had enough time to become *tahor*. "You go inside. I don't want you to miss the inauguration of the *Mizbeach*."

It was hard for Reuven to leave his father's side. He stood next to him, making sure not to touch him so that he wouldn't become *tamei*,[10] but he couldn't part from him.

"Go, Reuven," Binyamin repeated softly. "With Hashem's help, in a few more days we can come back here together. After I'm *tahor*, I'll come to bring two *korbanos Todah*: one because I was freed from slavery, which is like being released from prison, and the second for crossing the sea safely.[11] I'll take you with me. But now you should go in!"

Engrossed in their conversation, they didn't notice the Jew standing nearby, staring at them. Augustus smoothed out the new cloak that gave him a distinctly Jewish appearance and felt proud of the changes he had made in his life.

With slow steps, Reuven crossed the *Cheil*(2) and a moment later his slight figure was swallowed up in the *Azarah*.

*   *   *

The *Ezras Kohanim*(6) was filled with Kohanim dressed in white, faces glowing. The *mishmaros kehunah* still hadn't been fully organized, and because they were expecting so many *korbanos* to

---

10. *Bemidbar* 19:22.
11. Rashi, *Vayikra* 7:12.

be offered, *Beis Din* decided that until further notice all the Kohanim would serve in the Beis HaMikdash.

The *Ezras Yisrael*(4) was packed. Throngs of Jews stood crowded together, looking around with shining eyes. Elkanah was gently shoved into the crowd, trying to find a good spot. He was followed by a trail of five boys, and they positioned themselves opposite the *Ezras Kohanim*(6), where they had a good view of everything that was happening.

Zevulun tapped Elkanah lightly on the arm, trying to get his attention.

"Are they going to hold four lotteries today, like they always do?"[12]

"There will be four lotteries, but the Kohen who wins the first lottery will only get the privilege of arranging the Pyres and lighting them.[13] He won't remove the ashes. Yesterday, no sacrifices were offered, so there are no ashes on the *Mizbeach* today."

The children followed Elkanah's finger as he pointed to the *Mizbeach*. It was strangely empty and bright white in color. There was no *Tapuach*(87) in the center and no signs of blood on the corners.

"It's incredible!" breathed Yossi. "I've never seen the *Mizbeach* so new and...so bare!"

As he finished speaking, a Kohen briskly crossed the *Azarah* and washed his hands and feet in the new copper *Kiyor*(81).[14] His expression serious, he supervised the preparation of the three Pyres(88–90). Meticulously, he made sure that the work was being done properly, and then he lit the Pyres, one after the other.[15] The wood quickly caught fire and began to burn.

---

12. *Yoma* 22a.

13. Ibid.

14. Mishnah *Tamid* 1:4.

15. *Siddur Beis Yaakov, Ezras Kohanim* 25.

From another corner of the *Azarah*, Reuven watched the orange flames and swelled with pride. Just yesterday afternoon, the shipment of wood had arrived from Lebanon. Binyamin testified that the trees had been cut before the fifteenth of Av and had been checked by him personally. The Kohanim relied on him completely and just gave the wood a cursory check to make sure it was free of worms.

*   *   *

Some distance away, Elkanah was talking to his attentive students. "The *Mizbeach HaZahav*(83) was already inaugurated yesterday afternoon. From the *pasuk,* 'When Aharon kindles the lights in the afternoon, he shall burn the incense,'[16] we learn that the golden *Mizbeach* can only be rededicated when the *ketores* is offered in the afternoon.[17] Yesterday morning its construction was completed, and in the afternoon the *ketores* was offered on the new *Mizbeach*.

"Look at the *Shulchan*(80) next to the *Mizbeach*," Elkanah went on. "Do you see what's on it?"

The boys strained their eyes, trying to make out the distant shapes. On the *Shulchan*[18] stood the ninety-three utensils[19] that are used for the daily *avodah*. Today, very few of these utensils were made from gold or silver. Since there was not enough money in the Beis HaMikdash's coffers, most of the utensils were crafted from copper, as they were in the times of the Mishkan.[20]

"Maybe soon they'll collect enough money for those utensils, too!" said Yedidya, in a voice filled with hope.

*   *   *

---

16. *Shemos* 30:8.

17. *Menachos* 50a.

18. Mishnah *Shekalim* 6:4.

19. Mishnah *Tamid* 3:4.

20. *Shemos* 27:3.

At the sound of the *memuneh*'s cry, the large crowd hushed.

"Go and bring a lamb from the *Lishkas HaTelaim*(57)!"[21]

The announcement was familiar and beloved, yet at the same time it was new and exciting, different than always.

An enormous lamb[22] was led to the place where it would be slaughtered by the Kohen who had won that privilege.[23]

"The lamb was bought with money from the *machatzis ha-shekel* that was collected throughout the week from the people of Yerushalayim,"[24] Elkanah pointed out.

"What money will they use to buy the *korbanos* for tomorrow?" Zevulun asked worriedly.

"I'm sure that many of the people who came here today from the neighboring villages will place their half-shekels in the Shofar,"[25] Elkanah reassured him.

The Kohen who won the right to remove the ashes from the *Mizbeach HaKetores*(83) and the one who would be preparing the Menorah, entered the *pishpesh* and from there crossed into the *Heichal*(11). Together, they opened up its large gates(42) from inside.[26]

Tekiah, teruah, tekiah! The shofar was sounded as the gates of the *Heichal*(42) were opened.[27]

Inside, the Kohen approached the Menorah. The lights were extinguished. He climbed up the steps and looked inside, disappointed to find that that they were empty of oil. Until now, he had

---

21. Mishnah *Tamid* 3:3.

22. *Tosfos, Menachos* 87a, s.v. *she'govhan*.

23. Mishnah *Tamid* 3:5.

24. Mishnah *Shekalim* 4:1.

25. Ibid., 6:5.

26. Mishnah *Tamid* 3:6–7.

27. *Sukkah* 53b.

only heard about the great miracle; he had hoped that today he would see it for himself.

"Eight nights have passed already," he reasoned. "Last night pure oil arrived from the north. The miracle has ended, because starting today we can light the Menorah the natural way."

*   *   *

Outside, the *avodah* of the morning *korban Tamid* was swiftly being performed.[28] Even on an ordinary day, these tasks were performed with the utmost seriousness, but today there was a special sense of awe in Beis HaMikdash, a feeling of closeness to Hashem. It was the feeling of a father coming home after being far away for a long, long time.

With hearts full of love for their fellow loyal and devoted Jews, the Kohanim blessed the people, and when the *nesachim* wine was poured into the silver Funnel(101) that stood on the *Mizbeach*, the *avodah* was completed.

The sounds of the *Shir shel Yom* filled the air, quiet and hesitant at first, but gradually growing louder and stronger. The beautiful melody that had been silenced for so many months tugged at the chords deepest in the people's hearts and souls. Invisible prayers wafted in the air, filling every corner with yearning.

Although every Jew whispered his prayer in his own words, they all had the same request. "Please, Hashem, rest Your *Shechinah* in this House forever. Help us come close to You, and don't let anyone try to draw us away from the path of the Torah."

*   *   *

His eyes clouded with tears, Reuven edged his way through the sea of people. The experience has been unbelievably powerful,

---

28. The details of the *Tamid* offering are presented at length in the last seven chapters of the book *Seven Special Weeks*.

and he was eager to share it with his father. He found him on Har HaBayis, waiting on one of the stone benches.[29] On their way home, his father listened raptly to his vivid description and impressions of the day's *avodah*.

At home, there was a surprise waiting for Reuven.

On the large wooden table in the foyer lay two miniatures of the Beis HaMikdash.

"My sculptures! Where did you find them?"

His mother looked at him, surprised by how emotional he was. "They're yours? I didn't know! This morning, I decided to clear out the things that the Greek commander left behind when he escaped this house. Among his belongings I found these two lovely miniatures. I know you like wood carvings, but I never dreamed that you made these yourself! They're works of art!"

"Yehudah and I built them together while we were in the cave," Reuven explained, brushing a gentle hand over the tiny ladders. "I was so upset when they disappeared! I thought I would never see them again."

"It looks like you spent hours working on them," said his father, studying the exquisite structures in admiration. The two sculptures of the Beis HaMikdash were perfect, miniature replicas of the original.

"I did. Every time I felt sad and I missed the Beis HaMikdash, I took comfort in my carving knife and scraps of wood." Reuven had a dreamy look in his eyes. The memories were fresh and vivid.

"You can keep them in your room. It'll make a nice decoration," suggested his mother, picking up the models and heading there herself to put them away.

"No, it's not necessary!" Reuven's unequivocal tone made

---

29. Rashi, *Pesachim* 11b, s.v. *al gav.*

her stop in her tracks. She glanced at him in surprise, tying to understand his refusal.

"I'll give them to Yehudah," said Reuven, looking his mother in the eye. "Don't you understand? I don't need them anymore.

"When we didn't have the Beis HaMikdash, I found comfort in these miniatures. But today," Reuven's voice rose a notch and his cheeks flushed pink, "today I was in the real Beis HaMikdash. I was right there, together with Abba, who's free now. Who needs a wooden model when we have the real thing?"

*   *   *

We, too, have beautiful models, built perfectly to scale. We have breathtaking pictures, fascinating lectures and slideshows, and stories that move us to tears.

All these arouse in us a yearning for what was and hope for what will be.

Our Father in Heaven! We don't want miniatures, pictures, lectures, and stories. We want the real thing! We want the real Beis HaMikdash to descend from *Shamayim*![30] We want an end to the exile and the *tum'ah*; we want to witness the end of the *yetzer hara*.

Father, You are crying out to us, "*Shuvu eilai v'ashuvah aleichem* — Return to Me and I will return to you."[31]

We, Your children, respond, "After nearly two thousand years of exile, it's so hard for us to do *teshuvah*, but You are our Father, our King: '*Hashiveinu Hashem eilecha v'nashuvah chadesh yaminu k'kedem* — Bring us back to You, Hashem, and we shall return, renew our days as of old.'"[32]

When will we finally merit to see the King come home?

---

30. Rashi, *Sukkah* 41a, s.v. *iy nami*.
31. *Malachi* 3:7.
32. *Eichah* 5:21.

Key to Reference Numbers, Charts, and Maps of Sites in the Beis HaMikdash

> • *Most places and sites can be found on the main map on the inside back cover.*
> • *The locations of six chambers(71)(72)(73)(74)(75)(76) are unknown.*

Areas	אֲזוֹרִים
(1) *Har HaBayis* (Temple Mount)	הַר הַבַּיִת (1)
(2) *Cheil*	חֵיל (2)
(3) *Ezras Nashim* (Women's Courtyard)	עֶזְרַת נָשִׁים (3)
(4) *Ezras Yisrael* (Israelites' Courtyard)	עֶזְרַת יִשְׂרָאֵל (4)
(5) Platform (consisting of 4 steps)	דּוּכָן (4 מַדְרֵגוֹת) (5)
(6) *Ezras Kohanim* (Kohanim's Courtyard)	עֶזְרַת כֹּהֲנִים (6)
(7) *Mizbeach* (Altar)	מִזְבֵּחַ (7)
(8) *Beis HaMitbechayim* (Slaughtering Area)	בֵּית הַמִּטְבָּחַיִם (8)
(9) Between the *Ulam* and the *Mizbeach*	בֵּין הָאוּלָם וְהַמִּזְבֵּחַ (9)
(10) *Ulam* (Antechamber)	אוּלָם (10)
(11) *Heichal* (Temple Chamber)	הֵיכָל (11)
(12) *Kodesh HaKodashim* (Holy of Holies)	קֹדֶשׁ הַקֳּדָשִׁים (12)

Walls and Partitons	**חוֹמוֹת וּמְחִיצוֹת**
(13) Temple Mount Wall	(13) חוֹמַת הַר הַבַּיִת
(14) *Soreg* (lattice fence)	(14) סוֹרֵג
(15) Wall of *Azarah*	(15) חוֹמַת הָעֲזָרָה
(16) Wall of *Ulam*, Staircase, and Drainage Channel	(16) כֹּתֶל הָאוּלָם, הַמְסִבָּה וּבֵית הוֹרָדַת הַמַּיִם
(17) Wall of Compartments (*Ta'im*)	(17) כֹּתֶל הַתָּא
(18) Wall of *Heichal*	(18) כֹּתֶל הַהֵיכָל
(18a) *Lul* (window)	(18a) לוּל
(19) Two Curtains and the one-cubit passage between them, which divided the *Heichal* from the *Kodesh HaKodashim*	(19) אַמָּה טְרַקְסִין
Steps	**מַדְרֵגוֹת**
(20) 12 Steps ascending from *Cheil* to *Azarah*	(20) 12 הַמַּדְרֵגוֹת שֶׁבַּחֵיל
(21) 15 Steps ascending from *Ezras Nashim* to *Ezras Yisrael*	(21) 15 הַמַּעֲלוֹת
(22) 12 Steps ascending to *Ulam*	(22) 12 מַדְרֵגוֹת הָאוּלָם
(23) Staircase	(23) הַמְסִבָּה
(24) Drainage Channel	(24) בֵּית הוֹרָדַת הַמַּיִם
Gates	**שְׁעָרִים**
TEMPLE MOUNT GATES	**שַׁעֲרֵי הַר הַבַּיִת**
(25) Two Chuldah Gates	(25) שְׁנֵי שַׁעֲרֵי חֻלְדָּה
(26) Shushan Gate	(26) שַׁעַר שׁוּשָׁן
(27) Tadi Gate	(27) שַׁעַר טָדִי
(28) Kiponus Gate	(28) שַׁעַר קִפּוֹנוּס
AZARAH GATES	**שַׁעֲרֵי הָעֲזָרָה**
(29) Eastern Gate (entrance to *Ezras Nashim*)	(29) שַׁעַר הַמִּזְרָחִי
(30) Nikanor Gate (entrance to *Ezras Yisrael*)	(30) שַׁעַר נִקָנוֹר
(31) Two Side Doors on either side of Nikanor Gate	(31) שְׁנֵי הַפִּשְׁפְּשִׁים מִצְּדֵי שַׁעַר נִקָנוֹר
(32) Pyre Hall Gate (Music Gate)	(32) שַׁעַר בֵּית הַמּוֹקֵד (שַׁעַר הַשִּׁיר)

(33) The Women's Gate	שַׁעַר הַנָּשִׁים (33)
(34) Gate of the Sacrifice	שַׁעַר הַקׇּרְבָּן (34)
(35) Gate of the Spark (Yechonyah Gate)	שַׁעַר הַנִּיצוֹץ (שַׁעַר יְכׇנְיָה) (35)
(36) Two Western Gates	שְׁנֵי הַשְּׁעָרִים בַּמַּעֲרָב (36)
(37) Upper Gate	שַׁעַר הָעֶלְיוֹן (37)
(38) Gate of the Firewood	שַׁעַר הַדֶּלֶק (38)
(39) Gate of the Firstborn	שַׁעַר הַבְּכוֹרוֹת (39)
(40) Water Gate	שַׁעַר הַמַּיִם (40)

TEMPLE GATES — שַׁעֲרֵי הַבִּנְיָן

(41) Entrance to *Ulam*	פֶּתַח הָאוּלָם (41)
(42) Entrance to *Heichal*	פֶּתַח הַהֵיכָל (42)

Chambers — לְשָׁכוֹת

(43) Stone Chamber	לִשְׁכַּת בֵּית הָאֶבֶן (43)
(44) Minor Sanhedrin Chamber (on the Temple Mount)	סַנְהֶדְרִין קְטַנָּה — הַר הַבַּיִת (44)
(45) Minor Sanhedrin Chamber (in the *Ezras Nashim*)	סַנְהֶדְרִין קְטַנָּה — עֶזְרַת נָשִׁים (45)
(46) Nazirites' Chamber	לִשְׁכַּת הַנְּזִירִים (46)
(47) Wood Chamber	לִשְׁכַּת הָעֵצִים (47)
(48) *Metzora'im*'s Chamber	לִשְׁכַּת הַמְּצֹרָעִים (48)
(49) Oil Chamber	לִשְׁכַּת הַשְּׁמָנִים (49)
(50) Musical Instruments Chambers	לִשְׁכוֹת כְּלֵי הַשִּׁיר (50)
(51) Chamber for the Preparation of the *Kohen Gadol*'s flour-offering	לִשְׁכַּת עוֹשֵׂי חֲבִיתִּין (51)
(52) Chamber of Pinchas, Keeper of the Priestly Garments	לִשְׁכַּת פִּנְחָס הַמַּלְבִּישׁ (52)
(53) Chamber of Hewn Stone (seat of the Sanhedrin)	לִשְׁכַּת הַגָּזִית (53)
(54) Parhedrin Chamber (where the *Kohen Gadol* was sequestered for seven days before Yom Kippur)	לִשְׁכַּת פַּרְהֶדְרִין (54)
(55) Chamber of the Diaspora	לִשְׁכַּת הַגּוֹלָה (55)

(56)	The Pyre Hall	בֵּית הַמּוֹקֵד (56)
(57)	Chamber of Sacrificial Lambs	לִשְׁכַּת טְלָאֵי קָרְבָּן (57)
(58)	Chamber for preparation of Showbread (*Lechem HaPanim*)	לִשְׁכַּת עוֹשֵׂי לֶחֶם הַפָּנִים (58)
(59)	Chamber of the Receipts	לִשְׁכַּת הַחוֹתָמוֹת (59)
(60)	Small Pyre Chamber	בֵּית הַמּוֹקֵד הַקָּטָן (60)
(61)	Chamber of the Spark	בֵּית הַנִּיצוֹץ (61)
(62)	Salt Chamber	לִשְׁכַּת הַמֶּלַח (62)
(63)	*Parvah* Chamber	לִשְׁכַּת בֵּית הַפַּרְוָה (63)
(64)	Rinsing Chamber	לִשְׁכַּת הַמְּדִיחִין (64)
(65)	Avtinas Family Chamber	לִשְׁכַּת בֵּית אַבְטִינָס (65)
(66)	*Mikveh* of the *Kohen Gadol* above the *Parvah* Chamber	מִקְוֵה הַכֹּהֵן הַגָּדוֹל מֵעַל בֵּית הַפַּרְוָה (66)
(67)	*Mikveh* of the *Kohen Gadol* above the Water Gate	מִקְוֵה הַכֹּהֵן הַגָּדוֹל מֵעַל שַׁעַר הַמַּיִם (67)
(68)	Knives Chamber	בֵּית הַחֲלִיפוֹת (68)
(69)	Compartments	תָּאִים (69)
(70)	Attic	עֲלִיָּה (70)
(71)	Chamber (*Shekels* Chamber)	לִשְׁכָּה (לִשְׁכַּת הַשְּׁקָלִים) (71)
(72)	Chamber of Secrecy	לִשְׁכַּת חֲשָׁאִים (72)
(73)	Vessels Chamber	לִשְׁכַּת הַכֵּלִים (73)
(74)	Curtain Chamber	לִשְׁכַּת הַפָּרֹכֶת (74)
(75)	Chamber of the Sacrifice	לִשְׁכַּת הַקָּרְבָּן (75)
(76)	13 Shofar-chests for storing the Temple monies	שָׁלֹשׁ עֶשְׂרֵה הַשּׁוֹפָרוֹת (76)

Objects   חֲפָצִים

(77)	Rings to secure the animals for slaughter	טַבָּעוֹת (77)
(78)	Tables used for rinsing the flayed animals	שֻׁלְחָנוֹת בֵּית הַמִּטְבְּחַיִם (78)
(79)	Low Pillars for flaying the slaughtered animals	נַנָּסִין (79)
(80)	Two Tables near Altar	שְׁנֵי שֻׁלְחָנוֹת שֶׁלְּיַד הַמִּזְבֵּחַ (80)

(81) *Kiyor* (Washing Basin)	כִּיּוֹר (81)
(82) Two Tables in *Ulam*	שְׁנֵי שֻׁלְחָנוֹת הָאוּלָם (82)
(83) The Golden Altar (Incense Altar)	מִזְבֵּחַ הַזָּהָב (הַקְּטֹרֶת) (83)
(84) Menorah	מְנוֹרָה (84)
(85) Showbread Table	שֻׁלְחָן לֶחֶם הַפָּנִים (85)
(86) *Ehven HaShesiyah* (Location of the Ark in the First Temple)	אֶבֶן הַשְּׁתִיָּה (מְקוֹם הָאָרוֹן) (86)

Mizbeach (Altar)

מִזְבֵּחַ

(87) (*Tapuach*) Pile of Ashes	תַּפּוּחַ (87)
(88) Great Pyre	מַעֲרָכָה גְדוֹלָה (88)
(89) Second Pyre (for incense)	מַעֲרָכָה שְׁנִיָּה שֶׁל קְטֹרֶת (89)
(90) Pyre for Sustaining the Fire	מַעֲרָכָה לְקִיּוּם הָאֵשׁ (90)
(91) Kohanim's Footpath	מְקוֹם הִלּוּךְ הַכֹּהֲנִים (91)
(92) Main Ramp	כֶּבֶשׁ גָּדוֹל (92)
(93) Small Ramp on the East	כֶּבֶשׁ קָטָן מִמִּזְרָח (93)
(94) Small Ramp on the West	כֶּבֶשׁ קָטָן מִמַּעֲרָב (94)
(95) Window on the west side of Main Ramp, where disqualified burnt-offerings of birds were placed	חַלּוֹן (רְבוּבָה) (95)
(96) Circuit (*Sovev*)	סוֹבֵב (96)
(97) Southeastern Corner	קֶרֶן דְּרוֹמִית-מִזְרָחִית (97)
(98) Northeastern Corner	קֶרֶן מִזְרָחִית-צְפוֹנִית (98)
(99) Northwestern Corner	קֶרֶן צְפוֹנִית-מַעֲרָבִית (99)
(100) Southwestern Corner	קֶרֶן מַעֲרָבִית-דְּרוֹמִית (100)
(101) 2 Funnels for poured-offerings	שְׁנֵי הַסְּפָלִים (101)
(102) Red Line (*Chut HaSikra*)	חוּט הַסִּקְרָא (102)
(103) Northern Base	יְסוֹד צְפוֹנִי (103)
(104) Western Base	יְסוֹד מַעֲרָבִי (104)
(105) Southern Base	יְסוֹד דְּרוֹמִי (105)
(106) Passageway between Main Ramp and Altar leading under the Altar	לוּל (106)
(107) Fourth Pyre for Yom Kippur	מַעֲרָכָה רְבִיעִית שֶׁל יוֹם כִּפּוּר (107)

Glossary

The following glossary provides a partial explanation of some of the Hebrew and Aramaic (A.) words and phrases used in this book. The spellings and explanations reflect the way the specific word is used herein. Often, there are alternate spellings and meanings for the words.

AL KIDDUSH HASHEM: for sanctification of the Divine Name; martyrdom.

ALEICHEM SHALOM: the standard reply to SHALOM ALEICHEM.

AM YISRAEL: the nation of Israel.

AMAH/AMOS: cubit(s); a measure of approximately 21.5 inches, or 54 centimeters.

ANSHEI KNESSES HAGEDOLAH: "Men of the Great Assembly"; leaders of the Jewish people at the beginning of the second BEIS HAMIKDASH.

ARGAMAN: a type of dark red dye.

ARON KODESH: ark in which Torah scrolls are kept.

ASERES HADIBROS: the Ten Commandments.

AV BEIS DIN: the head of a Jewish court of law.

AVEIRAH/AVEIROS: sin(s).

AVNEIT: the belt that a KOHEN wears when performing the AVODAH.

AVODAH/AVODOS: service; the service performed in the BEIS HAMIKDASH.

AVODAH ZARAH: idolatry.

AVOS: the forefathers or Patriarchs — Abraham, Isaac, and Jacob.

AYELES HASHACHAR: a type of musical instrument.

AZARAH: the Temple courtyard.

BARUCH HASHEM: "Thank God!"

BARUCH HU U'VARUCH SHEMO: "Thank God, may His Name be blessed!"

BAVEL: Babylonia.

BEIS/BATEI DIN: Jewish court(s) of law.

BEIS HA-KNESSES/BATEI KNESSES: synagogue(s).

BEIS HAMIKDASH: the Holy Temple in Jerusalem.

BEIS/BATEI MIDRASH: Torah study hall(s).

BERACHAH/BERACHOS: blessing(s).

B'EZRAS HASHEM YISBARACH: "With God's help, may He be blessed."

BIGDEI KEHUNAH: special clothes worn by the KOHANIM when they performed the AVODAH.

BIKKURIM: the offering of the first fruits in the BEIS HAMIKDASH.

BLI NEDER: A phrase that changes a firm promise into an intention.

BNEI TORAH: men committed to learning Torah and keeping its laws scrupulously.

BRIS MILAH: circumcision.

CHACHAMIM: Sages.

CHAMETZ: leavened foods, prohibited during Passover.

CHANUKAS HABAYIS: dedication of the BEIS HAMIKDASH.

CHAS V'CHALILAH: "God forbid!"

CHAS V'SHALOM: "God forbid!"

CHASER: a short Hebrew month of only twenty-nine days.

CHATAS: a sin-offering.

CHAZAN: one who leads the congregation in the prayer service.

CHEIT HAEGEL: the sin with the Golden Calf (Exodus 32:1–6).

CHILLUL HASHEM: desecration of God's Name.

CHULLIN: something that is not holy.

CHUMASH: the Five Books of Moses.

DAYAN/DAYANIM: judge(s) in a Jewish court of law.

D'RABBANAN: by Rabbinic decree.

EIRUV TAVSHILIN: a Rabbinic device that allows performing work on a Festival that falls on Friday, for the following Sabbath.

EMUNAH: belief in God.

GEULAH: redemption.

GEDOLEI HA-DOR: great Torah scholars and leaders of the generation.

GEDOLEI TORAH: great Torah scholars.

GILUY ARAYOS: immorality.

HADLAKAS NEIROS: lighting the Menorah in the BEIS HAMIKDASH.

HALACHAH L'MOSHE MISINAI: a law not written in the Torah, but trans-
mitted to Moses at Mount Sinai.

HATAVAS HA-NEIROS: cleaning and preparing the Menorah in the BEIS
HAMIKDASH.

HEH: the fifth letter in the Hebrew alphabet.

HASHEM: God.

HODU LASHEM KI TOV, KI L'OLAM CHASDO: "Give thanks to God, for He
is good, for His kindness endures forever" (Psalms 118:1, 136:1).

ISSUR: prohibition.

KASHRUS: Jewish dietary laws.

KAVANAH: intent, concentration.

KAVOD: honor.

KEILIM: vessels.

KERIYAS SHEMA: the recital of SHEMA.

KESUVIM: "Writings," a section of Scriptures.

KETORES: the incense used in the BEIS HAMIKDASH.

KEVOD SHAMAYIM: the honor of Heaven.

KIDDUSH HA-CHODESH: sanctification of the new Jewish month.

KIDDUSH HASHEM: sanctification of God's Name.

KLAL YISRAEL: the Jewish people.

KLEI SHAREIS: vessels for service in the BEIS HAMIKDASH.

KODESH HAKODASHIM: the Holy of Holies; the innermost room of the
BEIS HAMIKDASH.

KOHEN/KOHANIM: member(s) of the priestly tribe; descendant(s) of Aaron,
brother of Moses.

KOHEN GADOL: the High Priest.

KORBAN/KORBANOS: sacrifice(s) or offering(s).

KORBAN EITZIM: offering brought in conjunction with wood donated for the MIZBEACH.

KORBAN MUSAF: offering brought on the Sabbath and Festivals.

KORBAN PESACH: the PESACH-offering.

KORBAN TAMID: the daily or "continuous" offering, brought twice a day in the BEIS HAMIKDASH.

KORBAN/KORBANOS TZIBBUR: communal offering(s).

KORBANOS TODAH: thanksgiving-offerings.

KRIYAS SHEMA: recital of the fundamental prayer which proclaims the unity of God.

KUZ: vessel into which were placed the old wicks of the Menorah in the BEIS HAMIKDASH.

K'VASIKIN: reciting the morning prayers at sunrise.

LASHON HAKODESH: lit., "the holy tongue,"i.e., Hebrew.

L'CHATCHILAH: from the outset, i.e., the preferable way of acting.

LECHEM HAPANIM: the twelve unleavened loaves of "showbread" in the BEIS HAMIKDASH.

LEVI/LEVIYIM: Levite(s); member(s) of the tribe of Levi.

LO YIHIYEH LECHA ELOHIM ACHEIRIM: "You must not have any gods of others" (Exodus 20:3).

LOG: measurement of liquid volume, equaling approximately 0.7 pints, or 0.3 liters.

MAARIV: the evening prayer service.

MACHATZIS HA-SHEKEL: half-shekel given to finance the AVODAH.

MALEH: a full Hebrew month of thirty days.

MANIM: plural form of the weight measure *maneh*. One *maneh* (a pound, or 425 grams) of KETORES was burnt every day in the BEIS HAMIKDASH.

MEGILLAS EICHAH: the Book of Lamentations.

MEI CHATAS: special water used to purify TUM'AS MEIS.

MEKABEL TUM'AH: something that is able to become TAMEI.

MEMUNEH: administrative appointed official(s) of the BEIS HAMIKDASH.

MIKVEH: a pool of water for ritual immersion and purification.

MINCHAH: the afternoon prayer service.

MINYAN: a quorum of ten men required for public prayer service.

MISHMAR/MISHMAROS: shift(s). See MISHMAROS KEHUNAH.

MISHMAROS KEHUNAH: divisions of KOHANIM, each serving a specific shift in the BEIS HAMIKDASH.

MISHMERES: shift. See MISHMAROS KEHUNAH.

MISHNAH: the codified Oral Law redacted by Rabbi Yehudah HaNasi.

MISYAVEIN/MISYAVNIM: Hellenist(s).

MITZVAH/MITZVOS: commandment(s); good deed(s).

MIZBEACH: altar.

MIZMOR: chapter from Psalms.

MOLAD: the time when the new moon appears.

MUSAF: the additional sacrifice in the BEIS HAMIKDASH pertaining to SHABBOS, ROSH CHODESH, and YAMIM TOVIM.

NACHAS: pleasure, satisfaction.

NAVI: "Prophets," a section of Scriptures.

NE'ILAH: a special prayer service added on YOM KIPPUR.

NESACHIM: poured-offerings upon the MIZBEACH.

NESHAMAH: soul.

NETILAS YADAYIM: the ritual washing of hands when eating.

NEVI'IM: "Prophets," a section of Scriptures.

NISUCH HA-MAYIM: the water-offering brought on SUKKOS.

OLAM HABA: the World to Come.

OLAM HAZEH: this world.

PARAH ADUMAH: the Red Heifer (Cow), whose ashes are burned and used for ritual purification.

PARASHAH: section from the Torah.

PASUK/PESUKIM: Scriptural verse(s).

PEREK: chapter.

PESACH: the Festival of Passover.

PEYOS: sidelocks.

PISHPESH/PISHPESHIM: small entryway(s).

RABBANIM: rabbis.

RABBOSAI: "My masters"; a respectful form of address.

REBBI: a Torah teacher.

RESHA'IM: evil people.

RIBBIS: interest on a loan.

RIBBONO SHEL OLAM: Master of the universe (God).

ROSH CHODESH: the first day of the Hebrew month.

SANHEDRIN: the high/supreme court in the time of the BEIS HAMIKDASH.

SEFER/SIFREI TORAH: Torah scroll(s).

SEUDAH: a festive meal.

SEUDAS HODA'AH: a meal of thanksgiving to God.

SHAATNEZ: the prohibition of wearing a garment that contains a mixture of wool and linen.

SHABBOS: the Sabbath.

SHACHARIS: the morning prayer service.

SHALOM ALEICHEM: "May peace be with you, "a traditional Jewish greeting.

SHAMAYIM: heaven; God.

SHAVUOS: the Festival of Pentecost, celebrated seven weeks after PESACH.

SHECHINAH: the Divine Presence of God.

SHECHITAH: kosher ritual slaughter.

SHERATZIM: low-creeping creatures.

SHEVET: tribe.

SHFICHUS DAMIM: murder.

SHIR SHEL YOM: section of Psalms sung in the BEIS HAMIKDASH for a specific day.

SHIUR: a lecture on a Torah topic.

SHLITA: a Hebrew acronym for "May he live long."

SHMAD: a time of decrees to force the abandonment of the Jewish religion.

SIFREI: possessive form of *sefarim* (scrolls).

SIMCHAS BEIS HASHO'EIVAH: the joyous celebration accompanying the drawing of the water for NISUCH HA-MAYIM.

SUKKOS: the Festival of Tabernacles.

TA'IM: compartments.

TAHARAH: ritually purity.

TAHOR: ritually pure.

TALMIDEI CHACHAMIM: Torah scholars.

TALMIDIM: students.

TAMEI/TEMEI'IM: ritually impure.

TAMID: see KORBAN TAMID.

TECHEILES: an aquamarine dye from the blood of a certain water creature.

TEFACHIM: "handsbreadths"; each *tefach* is approximately equivalent to 3.5 inches, or 9 centimeters.

TEFILLAH/TEFILLOS: prayer(s).

TEHILLIM: Psalms.

TEKIAH: straight trumpet blast.

TEMEI MEIS: TAMEI from a corpse.

TERUAH: staccato trumpet blast.

TESHUVAH: repentance.

TOLA'AS SHANI: a crimson dye produced from worms.

TREIF: not kosher.

TUM'AH: ritual impurity.

TUM'AS MEIS: ritual impurity from a corpse.

TZADDEIKES: righteous woman.

TZEIS HAKOCHAVIM: lit., "the emergence of the stars"; nightfall.

YAMIM TOVIM: Jewish holidays.

YASHER KOACH: "Good for you!"

YERUSHALAYIM: Jerusalem.

YETZER HARA: the evil inclination.

YOM KIPPUR: the Jewish Day of Atonement.

YUD: the tenth letter in the Hebrew alphabet.

ZECHUS: merit.

ZEMIROS: traditional hymns sung during the SHABBOS meals.

ZICHRONO LIVRACHAH: "May his memory be for a blessing."

ZUZIM: plural for the ancient silver coin, *zuz*.

ציון לנפש חיה

In loving memory
of a righteous woman

Yaffa Miriam Strauss ע"ה
daughter of יבלחט"א Rav Meir Snyder הי"ו

She raised and educated her children to
love of Torah and pure fear of Hashem
with much self-sacrifice and devotion.

She passed on to the World of Truth
on 22 Kislev 5758.

ת.נ.צ.ב.ה.

Memorialized by her children שיחיו

East

North   South

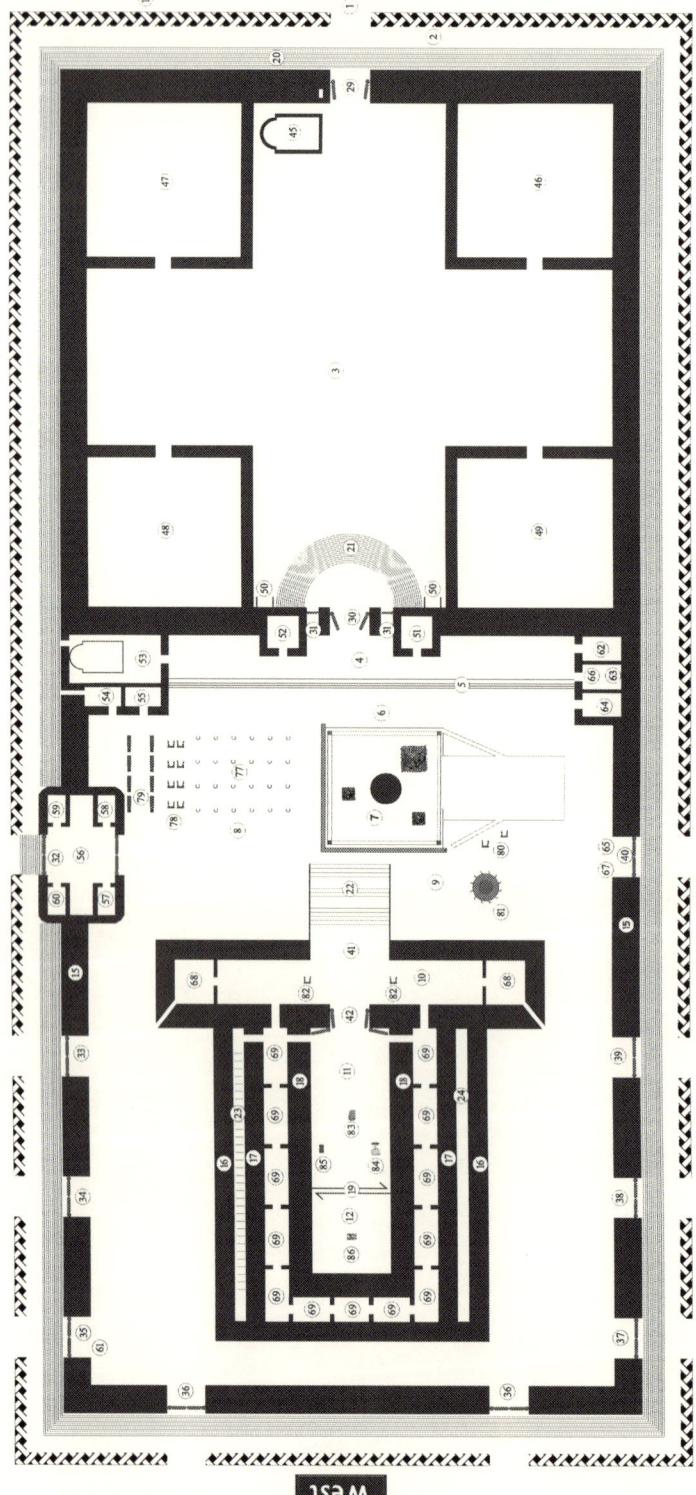

West

232

Made in the USA
Middletown, DE
04 November 2022

13892598R00149